WHAT
SHOULD
I DO?

WHAT SHOULD I DO?

Is it ever okay to be dishonest?
Is it wrong to enjoy violent video games, or to cheat on one's tax returns?
What does it mean to have equal opportunity to pursue some goal?
Does morality truly exist?

Life throws ethical questions at us every day. Some are momentous and difficult, while others are relatively trivial and easily worked out; still others lodge themselves in our heads and bother us for years at a time. We regularly encounter controversial issues (such as prostitution and racial profiling), everyday conundrums (Would I be wrong to take advantage of my teacher's forgetfulness? When should I allow my teenager to start dating?), and classic problems (When is war justified? Is suicide wrong?).

Philosophers have engaged with these questions for as long as there have been philosophers around, but most people have had no exposure to the wide variety of arguments and positions that they have offered. The website AskPhilosophers.org has sought to fill this void, bringing together a panel of distinguished philosophers who use their knowledge of the history of philosophy, as well as their own skills and ingenuity, to respond to questions sent in from all over the world. *What Should I Do?* is a collection of some of the most interesting questions about ethics to have appeared on the website during its first four years. It is a delightfully fresh book that will encourage readers to think a bit more deeply about the moral questions they frequently encounter, and will provide them with the tools to do so.

Alexander George teaches at Amherst College. Before arriving at Amherst, he was an undergraduate at Columbia, a graduate student at Harvard, and a junior research fellow at Wolfson College, Oxford.

WHAT SHOULD I DO?

*Philosophers on the Good, the Bad,
and the Puzzling*

EDITED BY
ALEXANDER GEORGE

WITH
ELISA MAI

OXFORD
UNIVERSITY PRESS

OXFORD
UNIVERSITY PRESS

Great Clarendon Street, Oxford OX2 6DP

Oxford University Press is a department of the University of Oxford.
It furthers the University's objective of excellence in research, scholarship,
and education by publishing worldwide in

Oxford New York

Auckland Cape Town Dar es Salaam Hong Kong Karachi
Kuala Lumpur Madrid Melbourne Mexico City Nairobi
New Delhi Shanghai Taipei Toronto

With offices in

Argentina Austria Brazil Chile Czech Republic France Greece
Guatemala Hungary Italy Japan Poland Portugal Singapore
South Korea Switzerland Thailand Turkey Ukraine Vietnam

Oxford is a registered trade mark of Oxford University Press
in the UK and in certain other countries

Published in the United States
by Oxford University Press Inc., New York

British Library Cataloguing in Publication Data

Data available

Library of Congress Cataloging in Publication Data

Data available

Typeset by SPI Publisher Services, Pondicherry, India
Printed in Great Britain
on acid-free paper by
Clays Ltd., St Ives plc

ISBN 978–0–19–958612–7

1 3 5 7 9 10 8 6 4 2

CONTENTS

CONTENTS

INTRODUCTION

The world ceaselessly throws problems our way.

Where can you buy a good bagel? How thick must the metal be so that the pressure cooker does not explode? Who left that chicken in my bedroom? When did Caesar cross the Rubicon? And so on. Many questions, such as these, merely require that we provide some information. But the world also confronts us with problems that call for appropriate *actions*. Every day, we need to act so as to avoid cars, earn money, make the meal edible. The goals in these cases are relatively clear.

But we are also regularly called to act in such a way as to . . . *do the right thing*. In some cases, this too can be straightforward: I should not steal library books, I should assign grades fairly, I ought not to step on this frog. It *can* be straightforward but, what with the curious curveballs life pitches us, it often isn't. I shall spare you examples, for surely your history has not spared you many bewildering, often painful, demands to act in the midst of a moral morass. How to decide what one should do in such circumstances? The goal of acting ethically is frustratingly elusive: What kind of goal is this, anyway? What does it mean to reach it? And how can we tell if we have?

Philosophy can be of some value here. Philosophers, after all, have been in the business of thinking about such matters since there have been any philosophers at all. By "some value" I do not mean that philosophy always, or even often, supplies answers. But even when it does not, it can provide some clarity and some guidance as one tries to make one's way through the usual cloud of confusions, fears, and aspirations that settles around our moral deliberations.

Unfortunately, few people have access to whatever help philosophy can offer. Philosophy hones one's powers of analysis and expands one's imagination, yet it is rarely taught in our schools. We live in a culture that values facts and techniques, or what passes for them, and derogates critical scrutiny and imaginative inquiry. It is little wonder that philosophy appears an esoteric enterprise at best, far removed from the vexing questions of daily existence that, in fact, provide the fodder for philosophical reflection.

AskPhilosophers.org (www.askphilosophers.org) was created to bridge, or at least to shout clearly across, the chasm in contemporary life between those with burning questions of a philosophical nature and those who have been trained in the skills and history of philosophy. Since its inception, the website has received thousands of questions from around the world, from young and old, from the educated to the barely schooled. And its volunteering professional philosophers have provided many thousands of responses. Not answers, but *responses*—a clarifying distinction, an interesting argument, some alternative positions, a pointer to pertinent reading—that might help refine further reflection.

This book, the second to be based upon AskPhilosophers.org,[1] focuses on questions about morality. These questions have been arranged here in ever expanding spheres of application and generality. They begin with ethical conundrums as they arise in the personal domain: questions about how to behave toward one's friends, members of one's family, those we love, and even toward oneself. The web of issues expands to include moral dilemmas faced in professional relationships, in our treatment of animals, in our use of the environment, and even in our relation to God. Broadening the sphere of application still further, we find questions about the morality of a nation's actions, such as its right to punish its citizens or to wage war against other nations. Finally, we consider some of the many questions people have about the nature of morality itself. One does not have to be a professional philosopher to find morality perplexing. One should do the right thing, of course, but is there always a right action? How does one tell what the right thing is? And what settles what is right?

Vexing as such questions may be, take a moment to consider what our lives would look like without them. As sad and flawed as our individual and collective histories of

---

[1] The first volume was *What Would Socrates Say? Philosophers Answer Your Questions about Love, Nothingness, and Everything Else* (Clarkson Potter, 2007). All proceeds from the sale of these books are donated to educational charities *via* the AskPhilosophers Fund (for details, see www.askphilosophersfund.org).

moral decision-making may be, their failures are as nothing in comparison to the brutish world that would result from our asking fewer questions, from our trying less hard to gain clarity about our moral obligations, from our giving up the struggle to figure out what we should do.

Alexander George
Amherst, Massachusetts

THE PERSONAL

CHILDREN

"My five-year-old daughter, after being told not to snitch on a friend, asked me why snitching is wrong. I didn't have a very good answer to give her. Why exactly is it wrong to snitch on a friend? In cases of minor mischief snitching on a friend would be disloyal, but just how far does our duty to our friends extend? What if I know my friend has done something wrong, and even though I wasn't involved she has asked that I remain silent on her behalf?"

Jyl Gentzler:

> I know that you're primarily interested in the more sophisticated question concerning the extent of our obligations to friends, but I'm stuck on childhood "snitching," or as it's known in my family, "tattling." "Don't be a tattle-tale," I'm often tempted to tell *my* five-year-old when she tells me of some minor indiscretion

1

of her fourteen-year-old sister. Why not? Didn't her sister do something wrong? And shouldn't wrongdoers be held to account? And isn't it my job as a parent to enforce all morally legitimate norms?

No, it is my job as a parent to do what is in my power to protect my children from unjustified harm and to help them to develop their capacities to live good, worthwhile, and morally decent lives. If they are being wronged by someone else and if they do not yet have the skills or authority to prevent that wrong, then I must intervene. But the usual situations that motivate tattling aren't like that. Most tattling is motivated by envy. Tattlers tend to regard moral norms as arbitrary rules enforced by parents that prevent them from having fun, and they don't want anyone else to get away with an illicit pleasure that they themselves would like to have. Alternatively, in a bout of sibling or classmate rivalry, many tattlers seek to present themselves to the local authority figure as "the good child" who knows and follows the rules, in contrast to those undeserving others. (Of course, *my* good child is never like this!)

Because I don't want to encourage these pictures of the point of moral norms (and also because tattling is really annoying), I am tempted to prohibit tattling. But I try to resist this temptation, because children often do find themselves at a loss about how to prevent injustices done against themselves and others, and a prohibition on tattling can seem like moral abandonment. So I try to resist the temptation to prohibit tattling, but

I also try not to give satisfaction to the envious tattler. "You need to tell your sister why her behavior upsets you. You don't know why it upsets you? Well, let's think about it. What is wrong with what she did? Anything, really? If not, then we shouldn't worry about it. It's not fair? Then maybe you can help your sister to see why it's unfair." And so on.

Of course, as my five-year-old will tell you, this picture of our domestic life is pure fantasy. Most of the time, in a desperate effort to maintain my own sanity, I take the much easier route: "Don't be a tattle-tale."

"My daughter, who is 14, wants to have a boyfriend. So far I haven't let her, because she seems just too young, and I'm afraid of what it might lead to. But is it right for me to control her in this way? Should I let her have a boyfriend?"

Nicholas D. Smith:

As a parent myself, my first reaction to your question is to say that it seems to me confusion about what is best for one's children is more the norm than the exception. Hardly a day goes by in my own case in which I don't feel profound uncertainty about how I should handle the wonderful and terrible project of parenting! So take whatever I say now with a boulder of salt, because, as you see, I regard myself as deeply in the dark about such things, at least as much as you feel you are.

3

It does seems to me, however, that there will prove to be increasing limits on the degree of control you will have over this issue, and so you should right now be thinking of something like an "exit strategy," by which I mean that you should be considering what you want your daughter to be able to think and do *for herself* (without any interference from you) in regard to her relationships with boys in the coming few years. Then, think of ways you can help her to achieve the sort of prudent and deliberative reactions that would eliminate the need for you to take protective measures at all. The fact is that you are already losing control of your daughter, and that process is going to continue—even escalate—in the coming years. For now, yes, you can simply prevent her from going out with boys. But very soon now, you will not be able to prevent much of what you fear most for her. She will have to do all that on her own.

So to answer your question with another question, I would ask you to consider whether a strict policy of not going out is, in your opinion, the best strategy for helping her to learn to be appropriately cautious and prudent in the ways she is going to need to be. Of course, at such an early age, there needs to be a *lot* that is off-limits. But is there no place, no time, no way at all that your daughter can begin now to have the sorts of independent experience with boys that will show her what she needs to be careful about, watch out for, and so on? Her interests in boys, I assure you, will not be eliminated or even diminished by adding the fascination of their being forbidden to her! How will she build the skills she will need for one of the most important (and often difficult) aspects of adult human life? *When* will you consider the process of slowly releasing the limits, all the while guiding and advising her? Because if you don't, she will simply void them and operate behind your back.

Increasingly, the only effective role you will be able to play in this is as a guide, advisor, and confidante—rather than as an absolute ruler. If you cling too long to the role you played when she was a small child, you risk losing the very influence she *needs* you to have during her adolescence and early adulthood. Don't make that mistake! Try now to begin to release your grip a bit, and remind yourself that allowing her to make some mistakes on her own is the only sure way to help her to learn how best to behave as an adult must do.

I hope you find this at least a little helpful. And now...can you give me some advice about my own children? I'm scared to death sometimes about them!

Jyl Gentzler:

I agree completely with all of Nicholas Smith's suggestions about parenting. I especially like his remarks about the importance of an "exit strategy." Our job as parents, after all, is to raise our children to be independent and responsible adults, but they can hardly acquire these skills if they are never able to make their own decisions and learn from their own, hopefully minor, mistakes.

At the same time, though, the high rates of teenage pregnancy and of women and children living in poverty remind us of the decisions that many fourteen-year-old girls will make when given the opportunity. This fact might suggest to us that many fourteen-year-old girls are not yet ready to make wise decisions for themselves. In such circumstances, it is our responsibility as parents to be paternalistic—to prevent them from making mistakes that will have lasting and negative implications for their lives. However, it might also suggest that being a mother is, in fact, given the circumstances in which they find themselves, the best chance that many young women will have of living a life with some meaning and significance, no matter how many challenges they will face as single mothers with no marketable skills.

And so, to Prof. Smith's difficult advice to help your daughter to develop the deliberative skills needed for wise independent decisions, I would add even more difficult advice. If you are inclined to restrict your daughter's activities because you are reasonably fearful of the consequences of the choices that she will make, see what you can do to make sure that the choice that you most fear isn't in fact the best choice for her. What, other than being with her boyfriend, does she most love to do? What sorts of talents does she have that she could develop? Does she have the opportunity to pursue these activities and develop these talents? Or is it boyfriend or boredom? And when she looks into her future, does she have any hope for fulfillment other than through young motherhood? If not, then even the wisest deliberator will make the choices that you most fear.

While I think that these are questions that we as parents must ask ourselves when we are tempted to shake our heads at the so-called "poor choices" made by teenagers, I really think that our society bears an even greater responsibility. There is only so much that parents who themselves have very few options can do to provide options for meaningful and fulfilling lives for their children. If we want our young citizens to avoid certain choices (teenage pregnancy, gang membership, etc.), we need to make sure that our society isn't structured so that these are the very best choices open to them.

"*Is it morally right to inculcate in your child religious belief when you do not firmly share that belief? Along the same lines, is there anything wrong with avoiding religious topics with your child, hoping that she will choose her own set of beliefs when she becomes more mature?*"

Louise Antony:

I should say right at the outset that I am not speaking as a specialist in ethics. I am a parent. My husband is also a philosopher. Our considered view is that, basically, one should not tell children things that one believes to be untrue. Perhaps there are exceptions— I'm not about to criticize the parents of a dying child who encourage the child to have hope. But if you're going to encourage a child to believe something you think is false, you need a really good reason. For one thing, it's imprudent: you risk your own credibility if the kid finds you out. In your case, what are your reasons for "inculcating" in your child a set of beliefs that you think are false?

Neither my husband nor I believes in Santa Claus, and therefore we did not tell our children that there was a Santa Claus. We didn't go out of our way to tell them that there *wasn't*, but neither of our kids seemed inclined to believe that there was. They talked about Santa Claus pretty much the same way they talked about Big Bird—they could enter into the pretense when it was fun to do so, but they weren't confused about the difference between reality and make-believe.

We also don't believe in God. We followed the same policy. Despite the urgent advice of many people whose business this wasn't, we did not feign religion "for the sake of our children." Whatever benefits there may be to belonging to a religious community—and my husband and I are prepared to admit that there are many—we just could not possibly have tried to persuade our children of something we believed to be false. There are always social benefits involved in believing what most people believe, or at least in acting as if one does. But if we want our children to resist peer pressure when it comes to drugs and sex, why not also belief?

Jyl Gentzler:

I have long been a non-believer, but I remember that when my first daughter was born, I too began to worry about the sorts of questions that are raised here. It's one thing for me to be a non-believer—I can't really help that, since the only thing that can give me a reason to believe in God would be evidence that suggests the existence of a God—but it's a separate matter whether I should try to inculcate a belief in God in my daughter. After all, I reasoned (in a panicky sort of way, overwhelmed by the sheer immensity of the responsibility that I had just taken on), I could be wrong, I've been wrong before, and if others are right in their belief that the existence of God is necessary for eternal bliss and non-belief in God is sufficient for eternal damnation, then perhaps it would be morally wrong for me to take a chance and doom my child to eternal damnation. I got over this worry pretty quickly, but now that I've just rehearsed it again, I'm beginning to panic again. What in the world is wrong with that reasoning?

Richard Heck:

> I don't think I'd want to say that it is permissible to "inculcate" one's children in a religion one doesn't accept. But that is strong and fairly loaded language.
>
> Suppose Alex and Tony are a white couple who have adopted two black children. They know that the church is and long has been the center of the black community, so they believe very strongly that it is important for their children to grow up in a black church. So they attend one of the local black churches and take their children, even though they themselves are not believers. I don't myself see anything impermissible about their doing so. In fact, it strikes me as admirable, even though it probably would not be consistent with their broader goals to convey their lack of belief to their children, since doing so could undermine their children's involvement in the church.
>
> So let's ask a more general question: Is it permissible to expose one's children *in a serious way* to religious life even if one is not oneself a person of faith? Here again, I don't see why it shouldn't be, and I can well imagine good reasons for wanting to do so. It doesn't have to be a fear of damnation.
>
> That isn't, of course, to say there is some *obligation* to expose one's children to religious life. That would be a much stronger claim.

LOVE AND SEX

"*I am having an affair with a married man who is my co-worker. I did not begin the affair; he pursued me. His wife does not know. I feel guilty about it, but at this point I am in love with him. He says that he loves me, but that he also loves his wife, because—although she is abusive and he feels no attraction to her—she was there for him when he was very ill two years ago. Are my actions unethical? If she doesn't know and I am truly in love with him, is it okay? Are his actions more unethical than mine?*"

Thomas Pogge:

Contrary to what you suggest, the fact that his wife does *not* know is probably sufficient to make the affair wrong. She stuck to this man throughout his serious illness, and thereafter, because she believed and still believes that they have a certain relationship with each other which she values highly. She does not in fact have such a relationship—her husband feels no attraction to her and is in love with you. If she knew that her life in fact lacks what she values highly, that her husband describes her to his lover as abusive, that he

11

stays with her only because she looked after him when he was ill—if she knew all this, then she would very seriously consider leaving her husband to try to build a new relationship of the kind she values. The deception deprives her of this opportunity and leads to her life's failing miserably in a respect that for her is very important, perhaps most important. The notion that she is not harmed so long as she does not know of this failure is patronizing and unresponsive to what *she* cares about: What she deems important is that she should have a meaningful relationship with her husband, not that she should have pleasant beliefs about this relationship.

(Imagine for a moment that the husband has a second secret lover as well, one who knows about you though you don't know about him or her. And imagine that he tells his second lover that he is very bored with you but stays with you because you might otherwise cause a scandal in the office. Wouldn't this make your life much worse even if you didn't know? Wouldn't you want to find out, despite the pain this would cause you, in order to have a chance to find a better relationship? If yes, then why assume otherwise about your lover's wife?)

Now, to be sure, I don't strictly know all this about the wife. I find it probable in view of what you wrote and in view of what I see around me in this culture. Perhaps I guess wrongly. Perhaps she loves him in a subservient, self-denying way that makes her care mainly about his happiness, not about their relationship or about whether her own life is fulfilled. If this were so (and the husband knew this), then *perhaps* it could be all right for him to have the affair and not tell her. He knows that she would want him to have this affair, if it makes him happy; and he knows that she would want to be there to serve him even if he loves someone else. So telling her would just cause her pointless pain. Not a likely scenario at all, in my view, but worth mentioning just to show that there might possibly be cases where having an affair without telling one's partner is morally all right.

The husband knows vastly more about his wife than you do. Nonetheless, you cannot simply rely on his expressed judgment that what he and you are doing is all right. (For one thing, he has a strong interest in misleading you and possibly deceiving himself on this point.) You need to judge whether what he tells you about her would make the affair all right. And you also need to judge whether what he tells you is true. In this case, what he has told you, even if true, does not justify your secret affair for the reason stated in the first paragraph. So I cannot see how the husband's conduct, or yours, could be ethical.

"On a Kantian view and a Utilitarian view, is homosexuality morally permissible?"

Allen Stairs:

The most relevant Kantian thought seems to be that we should never treat anyone, ourselves included, merely as a means and not also as an end. In Kant's view, *any* sort of sex outside marriage falls short on this score, including masturbation. This means that arguments against homosexuality based on Kant's views are likely to prove more than their proponent may have had in mind. But it's hard to credit the view that non-marital sex always amounts to nothing more than using someone simply for one's own pleasure; for one thing, good sexual partners care about their partner's pleasure and not just their own. And even if Kant were right, it's hard to see how marriage would magically solve the problem.

Which brings us to Utilitarianism. From that point of view, the fact that sex is a source of pleasure counts in its favor, and this applies no less to homosexual sex. Of course the Utilitarian will call on us to ask broad questions about consequences. Does homosexuality lead to more happiness than unhappiness overall? If *everyone* were homosexual, then the species might cease, but then again if *everyone* were a philosopher, we'd all die of starvation.

The most intriguing thing about this issue—the moral status of homosexuality—is that it somehow remains an issue. This tells us something about the charge around sexual matters, but not much else. It's hard to come up with serious, plausible arguments to show that there is something morally wrong with homosexuality.

"*Is prostitution wrong?*"

David Brink:

It's hard to believe that prostitution, as such, is wrong. There would seem to be cases in which this could be an unobjectionable voluntary exchange of services in which both parties are free to make the exchange. In such cases, it's not clear why engaging (or serving as) a prostitute would be any more objectionable than engaging (or serving as) a physical therapist. If so, there could be morally permissible cases of prostitution.

But, of course, many cases are not like this. In many places in the world, many prostitutes are forced into sexual slavery, against their will, at a young age. Even when prostitutes are not forced by others into prostitution, they may choose prostitution out of economic necessity, as someone might choose to sell a kidney out of economic necessity. Many who choose prostitution find themselves working for pimps who are abusive and don't allow easy exit from the profession. In conditions such as these, the sellers of sex may not be acting freely, or, if they are acting freely, they may not be acting with a fair opportunity to do otherwise. If so, there may be reasons not to purchase sex from such sellers.

So even if prostitution can be morally okay, it often isn't. This could be relevant to the *policy* question, which you do not ask, about whether prostitution should be legal and, if so, under what conditions. Of course, the fact that something can be done badly doesn't always mean that it should be forbidden. So the fact that sometimes prostitution is morally problematic doesn't imply that it should always be criminalized. Regulation is always an alternative to prohibition. But if moral problems attending an otherwise innocent transaction are common or systematic enough, this could be a reason for forbidding some or all sex trade, even if such a prohibition would capture some innocent transactions within its net. But that's a big and difficult policy debate.

"Is it worse to be unfaithful by action (having an affair) or by thought (fantasizing about another person)?"

Amy Kind:

You might want some way to assess each case on its merits. So you might think about what makes an affair wrong. Is it the betrayal of the spouse, or the effects that the affair has on the spouse? Some people might think: if my spouse had an affair, then even if I didn't know about it, and even if it made him behave nicer to me in the long run (perhaps because he came to appreciate me more), it would still be wrong because he would have betrayed me. On this view, the betrayal is bad independent of any effects it has. But some people locate the very badness of the betrayal in its effects: my spouse treats me poorly, spends our money indiscriminately, maybe other people treat me differently as a result of the affair (they might look down on me and think I'm a fool), and so on. And of course, maybe the affair leads to a breakdown of the marriage, which has all sorts of devastating consequences.

Now, regardless of whether you think that the affair is wrong just in virtue of its being a betrayal or is wrong because of its bad effects, you can think about the "fantasy affair" the same way. (I'm here assuming that the fantasy affair isn't just an occasional stray thought, but is a full-blooded fantasy, one that becomes a preoccupation of sorts.) Does the fantasy affair have bad effects on your spouse? Does the fantasy affair itself count as a betrayal? Depending on your answers, you can compare its badness to the badness of an actual affair.

In my own view, both the affair itself and the fantasy affair count as betrayals, and betrayal is a bad thing in and of itself, independent of any bad effects it might have. But I hope the above gives you something of a framework to think about your question (and perhaps it also gives you something to keep your mind occupied, rather than leaving it free to wander in fantasy).

"Why is it considered morally wrong for a man or a woman to have a romantic or sexual relationship with someone significantly younger?"

Richard Heck:

I don't know that it is considered morally wrong, simply in virtue of the age difference. It's true, to be sure, that people are often inclined to speculate about the reasons a younger person might be involved with an older one, but such speculation is typically just gossip. It's also true that such relationships can pose certain kinds of challenges to the people involved. But, as I said, I don't know of any general reason to regard such relationships as immoral *simply* in virtue of the age difference.

Of course, it is another matter when we are talking about minors, but I don't take the question to concern that kind of relationship.

Nicholas D. Smith:

I generally agree with what Richard Heck said, but would add a proviso: I am inclined to think that there is something (not without exceptions, of course) to the suspicion that people tend to have when they consider relationships between people who are unusually far apart in age. Reciprocation is important to any relationship. People very different in age can, of course, enjoy fully reciprocal relationships. But differences in age usually also tend to be associated with differences in perspective, in interests, in worldly wisdom, and in lots of other areas that are profoundly important in relationships. So, when one tends to be suspicious of romantic relationships between people

18

of very different ages—and all the more so when one partner is very young—it may well be because one is not unreasonably uneasy at the thought that the relationship itself may be very unequal and unreciprocal.

And there's another reason that doesn't seem to me to be mere gossip: I would hazard a guess that most such relationships pair much older men with much younger women, though of course there are exceptions to this generality. Given the prevalence of sexism, such relationships seem to raise reasonable suspicions that they are embodiments of widespread sexist attitudes towards women, who suffer disproportionately from discrimination as they age, and for whom standards of attractiveness (including youthful appearance) are especially oppressive. So I don't think these suspicions are always *just* prejudice and speculative gossip. But I also think that each relationship is unique, and that suspicions based on generalities can never be secure guides by which to judge others.

" *Is extreme (very violent) consensual sado-masochism morally wrong? If so, should it be against the law to cause injury by this practice? Or would it be a "private" matter?* "

Peter S. Fosl:

The old principle of liberty famously formulated by John Stuart Mill—that one can do what one likes so long as it doesn't harm others—is challenged by this sort of issue. What if someone consents to being harmed or even asks to be harmed? Can one consent to be another's slave? My view is that liberty has been found to be such a good thing that it should be maximized. But it does have limits. Sometimes those limits have to do with advancing collective, social, or political goods, like education and equality. Sometimes they involve protecting people from themselves. Why should people be protected from themselves? Because our actions towards ourselves as well as towards others are not matters of simple will disconnected from the structures of character, coercive power relationships, psychological manipulation and pathology, deceit, and plain old stupidity.

On this score, I vote for maximal sexual liberty. And so I support undermining compulsory heterosexuality, compulsory binary relationships, and fixed sexual and gender identities. I find limited sado-masochism permissible. But experience and history suggest that extremely violent relationships are likely pathological, abusive, exploitive, sexist, and deceptive. For these reasons, sado-masochistic practices that lead to serious injury (broken bones, loss of life, hospitalization, trauma) should be prohibited by law. Games of Russian roulette and "consensual" slavery are impermissible for similar reasons.

ABORTION

"It takes two to tango, so to speak, and thereby conceive a child. And down the line, guys are legally just as responsible for children as women are. Shouldn't a guy have some say in deciding whether his partner will have an abortion?"

Lorraine Besser-Jones:

It is true that abortion debates rarely, if ever, take into account the man's perspective. People who oppose abortion believe that aborting a fetus is wrong regardless of whether the man (or woman) is in support of so doing. Most people who believe that abortion is morally permissible believe that it is the woman who has the right to make the decision on her own—even if that decision conflicts with the man's wishes.

Why do men get left out of the debate? Because it isn't clear what rights they have that could outweigh the rights of the other parties involved. The central rights at stake in abortion debates are the woman's right to autonomy (that includes the right to decide what happens to her body) and the fetus' right to life (or lack thereof). These two rights—the right to autonomy and the right to life—are generally taken to be the

21

most central of all of our rights, and neither the man's right to autonomy nor the man's right to life are jeopardized by the prospect of an abortion. This is why men get left out of the abortion debate.

While some people believe there is a right of "procreative liberty," which includes the right to reproduce, or at least, the right to make decisions regarding reproduction, we wouldn't want to say that the man's procreative liberty overrides a woman's right to autonomy, for (among other reasons) this would legitimize non-consensual sex. So, as your questions suggests, it seems that this is an instance where men are stuck: they bear responsibility for the fetus, yet do not have the right to make decisions about its future.

Jyl Gentzler:

Is it fair that fathers who have had no say in whether a fetus is brought to term should be held legally responsible for meeting the needs of their progeny? This, it seems to me, is a legitimate moral question.

But I wonder whether we are looking at the situation in the right way. It seems to me that so long as fathers do not take on an equal share of the responsibility for meeting the needs of their progeny, the decision whether to abort a fetus (if such a decision is to be made available to anyone) must be given to women. For, as a matter of fact, and whether fair or not, most women bear the primary responsibility for meeting the needs of their children. It seems to me that if men wish to be granted the right to play an equal role in deciding whether a fetus for which they are responsible is brought to term, they must also be willing to play an equal role in meeting the needs of their children.

" *Many people reject the death penalty on the grounds that the mere possibility of mistakenly executing an innocent person is too big a risk to take. What would these people say about abortion? After all, if no one is certain when life begins, don't we run the risk of mistakenly aborting an innocent person?* "

Allen Stairs:

I sometimes call this the "Ronald Reagan argument"—President Reagan was fond of a version of it that, as I recall, had to do with a man in a ditch who might or might not be dead. That also raises a preliminary issue. The question presumably isn't whether the fetus is biologically alive; for surely it is. The question, rather, is what this living being is. One common way of putting it is to ask whether the fetus is a person, a being with the same moral standing as you or me. And so I'll put what follows in those terms.

The first thing that strikes me is that there's a glitch in the analogy. In the execution case, the being we execute is unquestionably a person, a person who is possibly innocent. In the abortion case, the being is possibly a person, though if a person, then an innocent one.

This hardly settles the matter, of course. The reply might be that in either case, we run the risk of taking the life of an innocent person; the position of the word "possible" simply locates the source of the risk. But that's too simple. In the typical execution case, what we worry about getting wrong is a matter of fact; the person either committed the crime or didn't, and the concern is that we may be mistaken about which is the case. The abortion case is different. Whether or not a fetus is a person seems to be what someone once called an essentially contested question: there may be no straightforward fact to be had. Fetuses are like paradigm cases of persons in some ways, and very unlike them in others. A glance at the history of the debate makes it clear that two people can agree about all the background facts (genetic make-up, brain development, etc.) and still disagree about whether the fetus is a person. It's harder to cook up a case like that when the question is whether someone committed murder.

There's another difference: the thought of executing an innocent person makes our blood run cold when we think about it from the victim's point of view. Imagine yourself knowing full well that you've been convicted of a murder that you didn't commit, and that you're about to have your life taken away from you on the basis of a mistake. It's a horrifying prospect. Abortion holds no such horror from the fetus's point of view, because the fetus doesn't have a point of view. It has no conception of its future, let alone of itself.

Just to be clear, my point isn't to settle the abortion issue. After all, newborns don't have anything like the developed point of view of a paradigm person, but infanticide still strikes us as wrong. The point is simply that the Ronald Reagan argument, in its various versions, is too quick.

" *How can abortion be so easily accepted in a civilized society? Sure, it is important that women have control over their bodies, but since a newborn is a separate entity—a new person completely—so is a fetus. What gives any person the right to kill someone else so that they can live the way that they want?* "

Allen Stairs:

There are plenty of hard issues about when and whether abortion should be allowed, but the particular argument you're offering won't work. You say that a typical newborn is a person, and you go on to conclude that a fetus is a person. But this simply doesn't follow. It's perfectly consistent to think that, say, a two-week-old embryo isn't a person, i.e., a being with the same sorts of rights that you and I have, even though, other things being equal, this embryo will eventually become a person.

Jasper Reid:

There's something else in your question that doesn't seem quite right. Allen Stairs queries your claim that the fetus is "a new person"; for my part, I have some misgivings about the claim that it's "a separate entity." In what sense is the fetus separate from the mother? In the literal sense of the term, it blatantly *isn't* separate from her. It's inside her own body, and connected to her body through the placenta, no more separate from her than are her liver or kidneys. You might say: okay, but it's separate in the sense that it has the *potential* to survive in separation from her, as her liver and kidneys do not. But, for a fetus in the early stages of development, that's not true either. Many countries permit abortion, but—except in really extreme cases where the mother's life is endangered—only up to a certain time, that time being principally determined by the stage of development at which a fetus becomes capable of surviving outside the mother. Prior to that time, the living fetus not only isn't separate from the mother, but *cannot* be. You might say: fine, but what the fetus does have, even at that early stage of development, is, as it were, the potential to develop the potential to survive in separation from the mother. If left unmolested, it will eventually develop that potential, and then finally actualize it in birth. And that much does seem true.

Of course, this doesn't answer the moral question, but merely recasts it in a new form. Indeed, I fear that I may have been indulging here in the sort of subtle nit-picking that tends to give philosophers a bad name. But it's important to get the question straight before we can hope to answer it. The issue becomes one of whether this potential potential is sufficient to confer a right to life onto the fetus. Life by itself is not enough to establish a right to life. A person's kidney is alive, for instance, but it surely doesn't have a right to life. If one of a woman's kidneys is troubling her, it'll just be removed and tossed in the bin while she carries on with the other, and no one will bat an eyelid over that loss of life. As I've indicated, the thing that sets the fetus apart from the kidney is its future potential. Is that enough of a difference to give it such an enormously elevated moral status? Some would say that it is, others would say that it isn't, and there are strong feelings on both sides. Unfortunately, not being an ethicist myself, I don't feel qualified to answer that question for you.

Peter Smith:

Allen Stairs rightly queries the claim that the fetus is already a new person. Killing an early fetus is not straightforwardly killing a person—it is at most killing something that would otherwise become a person. Still, you might be tempted to say (indeed, many people do say) that killing a potential person is as bad as killing a fully-fledged person.

Well, I disagree. But just asserting a disagreement is hardly very interesting. So what sort of grounds could I give to support my position? What sort of grounds

27

could you give for yours? At this point, we might be tempted to bandy about very general principles about the morality of killing or the "right to life" which are supposed to settle things one way or the other. This might help. But more likely, it will just shift the debate from a clash of intuitions about abortion to a clash of intuitions about these more general principles about killing and we will find ourselves going around in circles. What to do?

I think it can help to set our thinking about abortion not just in the wider context of principles about killing, but in the wider context of what we think about other early fetal deaths which happen naturally, by accident, or by misadventure. It does seem to be a notable fact that while a natural miscarriage in the very early weeks of a pregnancy may be, for some mothers, a misfortune, very few people regard it as the moral equivalent of the death of a newly born baby. Suppose a young woman has accidentally become pregnant, to her distress, and then a couple of weeks later a very early test shows that she has had a natural miscarriage. She feels much relieved and cheered at the outcome. Her girlfriends even buy her a drink to celebrate. Very few of us would morally condemn the woman or her friends for their feelings! Very few would regard the woman as morally on a par with a mother who cheerfully celebrated the death of an inconvenient baby.

Here's another notable fact. It is estimated that 25 percent of all pregnancies are miscarried by the fourth week. Yet no one seems to campaign for medical intervention to reduce that figure in the way that they might campaign to raise money to reduce a high rate of child deaths in a developing country. We let nature take its course, even if that course involves the spontaneous miscarriage of a very large number of "potential people."

You can probably multiply such examples for yourself. And they do suggest that—when we turn our attention away from the intentional causing of an abortion to other natural cases of early fetal death—we do not in general seem to regard the death of an early fetus as morally on a par with the death of a child. (I'm not saying we think of it as entirely insignificant, just that we seem to give the death increasingly more weight as the fetus develops.)

But now the question obviously arises: if in practice we do not believe that the natural death of an early fetus is the moral equivalent of the natural death of a fully-fledged person, and if we are happy to retain that general view on reflection, then why should we think that the intentional killing of an early fetus is the moral equivalent of the intentional killing of a fully-fledged person? If the natural death of a potential person doesn't matter as much as the natural death of a child (think again of all those spontaneous miscarriages), then why should the unnatural death of a potential person be thought of as particularly grave, as the moral equivalent of infanticide? I, for one, find it difficult to see any reason for treating the gravity of the natural and unnatural deaths very differently.

There are, of course, various further things that might be said here (but not in the confines of a short answer!). But at least we have a hopefully illuminating suggestion about how to start thinking about abortion. Try thinking first about the moral weight you actually do give to other kinds of embryonic/fetal deaths at various stages, in particular to natural or accidental deaths. Consider whether you are content to rest with those views you have. Now try to make your moral views about the level of seriousness of causing fetal death fit together consistently with those views about the seriousness of natural and accidental deaths.

EMOTION

"*Can people be held responsible for their emotions? Why or why not?*"

Nicholas D. Smith:

I think adults can be held responsible for their emotions, on the grounds that we have good evidence to think that people can learn to feel the right emotions at the right times for such emotions (and, conversely, not to feel the wrong emotions when it is inappropriate to feel those emotions). Few of us are masters of this, of course, but that doesn't mean that we can't (or shouldn't) be faulted when we feel inappropriate emotions, or don't feel appropriate ones.

Jyl Gentzler:

I think the idea of being held responsible for our emotions is puzzling at first. It seems that in order to be responsible for X, it has to have been up to me whether to X. Actions seem to be good candidates for responsibility, since they seem to be something over which I have control. When someone annoys me, I can choose whether to utter some caustic remark or instead bite my tongue. But what about my feeling annoyed in the first place—do I have any choice about that? And if not, then can I really be held responsible for this emotional reaction?

Aristotle is very helpful on this point. While it is true that on the particular occasion on which you feel the emotion, you can't help but feel it, you are nonetheless responsible for your emotion since you were responsible for becoming the sort of person who feels this sort of emotion. Being susceptible to bad emotional responses (i.e., having a bad character) is, on Aristotle's view, like being sick:

For neither does a sick person recover his health [simply by wishing]; nonetheless, he is sick voluntarily, by living incontinently and disobeying the doctors, if that was how it happened. At that time, then, he was free not to be sick, though no longer free once he has let himself go, just as it was up to someone to throw a stone, since the principle was up to him, though he can no longer take it back once he has thrown it. Similarly, then, the person who is [now] unjust or intemperate was originally free not to acquire this character, so that he has it voluntarily, though once he has acquired the character, he is no longer free not to have it [now].

(*Nicomachean Ethics* III 5, 1114a12–23)

Aristotle believes that we can train our emotional responses by forcing ourselves to act in the right way. Even if our emotions rebel at first, we will eventually come to take pleasure in the right actions. The contemporary philosopher Daniel Dennett suggests another strategy for taking control over our emotions:

Suppose I know that if I ever see a voluptuous woman walking unescorted in a deserted place I will probably be overcome by lust and rape her. So I educate myself about the horrors of rape from the woman's point of view, and enliven my sense of the brutality of the crime so dramatically that if I happen to encounter such a woman in such straits, I am unable to do the awful thing that I would have done otherwise.

(*Elbow Room*, p. 134)

As Dennett assumes here, we can control at least the force of some of our bad emotional reactions through education. Since, dear reader, you are one of the fortunate for whom being more or less educated is up to you, you can be rightly held responsible for many of your emotional responses.

" *Courage is considered a virtue, but it's often defined in the dictionary as the "lack of fear." How can the "lack of fear" be a virtue? Simply not experiencing the emotion of fear doesn't seem terribly virtuous, and anyway, we don't have much control over the emotions we experience or don't experience.* "

Peter Smith:

The dictionaries you are consulting are wrong. Courage is not a matter of lack of fear. It is a matter of not letting even justified and appropriate fear stand in the way of doing the right thing, such as rescuing your injured friend from a burning building, standing up for the innocent man in the face of the baying mob, and refusing to betray the whereabouts of the resistance fighter. Not to feel fear of the fire (or the mob, or the Gestapo, or whatever) would be a sign of a kind of reckless madness, not of virtue. The virtue of courage comes in knowing when it is appropriate to let fear guide your actions and when you have to master it—and in being able to do so.

" *Today I had a big fight with my sister, and we were both sulking, upset and angry. I told my father that*

I was really hurt and he said that it is not worth being hurt when there are people right now in Israel, Lebanon, Sudan, the Congo, and elsewhere who have lost their homes, family members, and futures in the blink of an eye. And that if you told those people there were two girls in New Jersey who got to go to school every day, who had a comfortable house, an intact family, and never had to worry about food or money or safety, they would think it was ridiculous how sad and hurt and angry we were being. I understand my dad's point. He is saying, firstly, that we should be grateful for what we have and not bitter about the small things that are not going well, and, secondly, that we should think of our problems in light of what the rest of humanity may suffer. But can these thoughts ever really act as consolation? Does the fact that something worse exists somewhere else make a bad thing less bad? It seems that you can't fully put emotions in perspective."

Thomas Pogge:

That something much worse exists does not make a bad thing less bad. But it may well make you feel much less bad about it. And that's what a consolation is, really: something that makes you feel less bad. In this case, it can be achieved by gaining a broader perspective—by seeing the wrong you suffered in comparison to other wrongs (and, I might add, also in comparison to all the good times you have had, and will have again, with your sister). However big and irreparable the hurt felt at the time, it's really just a blip on a larger canvas.

Miranda Fricker:

What is it to keep one's emotional reactions in proportion? There is a philosophical issue here that seems worth raising: emotional reactions are not simply sensational reactions to the world. They can be cognitive reactions as well. Emotions can sometimes tell one things about the world that one's beliefs aren't registering. Perhaps your anger and upset about the argument with your sister contained a cognitive response that was appropriate to the scale of the argument with your sister, in which case the emotional content in itself should not be changed by the thought that there are many situations in this world that would be infinitely more upsetting and difficult to bear.

The advice that one should keep one's emotional responses in proportion—making sure the cognitive content is correct, if you like—might sometimes require one to let it go, but equally it might require one to stand by the upset and conclude that the argument one had this morning was indeed really upsetting. If so, one needs some other way forward besides remembering how much worse things could be: talking it over with one's sister, explaining why one was so hurt, asking if she felt the same, and so on. Keeping emotions proportionate to the facts cuts both ways.

SINCERITY

" *Are there situations in which it is morally OK to be dishonest? What if telling the truth to someone would hurt his feelings very badly?* "

Peter S. Fosl:

I think there are times when it's better to conceal the truth. Part of wisdom in ethics involves not just being truthful but knowing *when* and *how* the truth should be told. Mind you, there are good reasons for being maximally truthful. But they do not count in every case, and sometimes other considerations trump them.

Nicholas D. Smith:

Different general approaches to ethics may provide different answers to this question. Speaking very broadly, there have been three basic approaches to ethical theory. Kant (and others like him, called "deontologists") will argue that the correct way to view ethics is by formulating rules that may be applied universally. In this approach, dishonesty will always be wrong—though in some cases it might be the lesser of two evils. J. S. Mill (and others like him, called "consequentialists" or, more narrowly, "Utilitarians") will approach ethical questions with a view to what consequences will flow from the act in question (or else from the rules they formulate that will tell us how to act). In this approach, lying can sometimes be good because it will have better consequences, all things considered, than telling the truth. Aristotle (and others like him, called virtue theorists) will say that the primary bearer of value is the character of the agent, and not the actions the agent performs. For a virtue theorist, lying would be OK (or even the right thing to do) when and if a virtuous person would lie in that situation.

A good example of a discussion on this very point, from a virtue theoretical point of view, can be found in Plato's *Republic* Book I (331a—c). Plato claims there that it would be wrong to tell the whole truth to someone who was out of his mind (and who might, therefore, react to the truth in an irrational or possibly dangerous way). For a virtue theorist, one-size-fits-all moral principles will always have exceptions, and the sort of case you seem to be worried about may be of this sort. For such exceptional cases, according to virtue theory, good ethical judgment will always be required and can only come from adequate training and habituation.

In the final game of the 2006 World Cup, French midfielder Zinedine Zidane headbutted Italian defender Marco Materazzi for insulting him. In the aftermath, Zidane apologized in an interview with a

French television station but added that he didn't regret his actions. Can one coherently apologize for an action yet not regret that action?"

Matthew Silverstein:

An apology is an acknowledgment of responsibility and an expression of regret. However, the words "I'm sorry" are not always meant to convey an apology. When I tell a friend who has recently lost a close relative that I'm sorry for his loss, I'm not accepting responsibility or expressing regret for anything I've done. I'm merely expressing my feelings of sympathy. So whether Zidane was inconsistent depends on precisely what he said. It would be perfectly consistent for Zidane to express sympathy with the French people for what happened but deny that he regrets his action.

Of course, the problem with this is that most of us feel that Zidane should do more than say "I'm sorry" out of sympathy. He did something wrong, and he should say "I'm sorry" out of regret. He should, in other words, *apologize*.

Let's see what he *did* say. According to the BBC's translation, it went like this: "It was inexcusable. I apologize. But I can't regret what I did because it would mean that he was right to say all that." If that's an accurate translation, then clearly Zidane's apology was insincere. His proviso ("But I can't regret what I did") pretty much ensured that the apology would not be taken seriously. And so, to answer your question, if the

BBC translation is a good one, then there *is* something problematic about what Zidane said. It is inconsistent to say: "I apologize for what I did, but I don't regret what I did."

While we're on the subject, there's something else puzzling about Zidane's comment. He says that he can't regret his action "because it would mean that he [Materazzi] was right to say all that." But it doesn't mean that at all. If someone is saying inappropriate things to me (on or off the pitch), I do not acknowledge that he is right to say them by refusing to respond violently!

"*I find myself particularly concerned with the concept of hypocrisy. If Dr Johnson tells me not to smoke because smoking is bad for my health, yet Dr Johnson himself is a chain smoker, does that reduce his credibility? Why does the United States condemn other countries for human rights violations, when it violates the rights of its own prisoners? What about the judge who sentences someone to 10 years in jail for a crime that, secretly, he also commits?*"

Thomas Pogge:

A nice triplet of examples! Let's say that a person is hypocritical just in case s/he (a) publicly endorses a normative position (such as a moral principle or value or norm or end) as valid for everyone and also (b) deliberately contravenes this normative position.

Your physician may not be hypocritical on this account. Yes, he deliberately contravenes the instruction he gives to you. But he may not be endorsing this instruction as valid for all. Here are some possibilities: (1) He endorses the instruction as valid only for those who seek to be in good health, he assumes that you are among these people (why else would you be going to the doctor?), and he is not himself among them. When charged with hypocrisy, he then responds that he is no more hypocritical than a travel agent who advises you to spend a few days in Paris even though she would never want to travel overseas. (2) He may endorse the instruction as valid only for those who are still young or as valid only for those for whom quitting would not be a nightmare. He may then deflect the charge of hypocrisy by pointing out that he would follow the instruction himself if his circumstances were relevantly similar to yours. You may ask him, "So why did you smoke when you were my age?" Even if his reply is that he foolishly continued smoking even though he knew the health risks, this does not necessarily, I think, make him a hypocrite. People change their views, and it's not necessarily hypocritical to express a new view one genuinely believes in even if one also acted against this view in the past (e.g., it is not hypocritical for a genuinely reformed ex-racist to speak up against racism now). So the above definition must be refined by adding

(c) that there was not a genuine change in the person's normative view between the two events.

Your second case can be made a little sharper by focusing on specific US officials. Imagine someone who works for the US State Department and is asked to write a human rights report about Indonesia. Her report, endorsing certain human rights and condemning the Indonesian military for systematically violating them, is accepted and published. I don't think this makes the official herself hypocritical: She is not involved in US human rights violations and may even do what she can to reduce them—say, by including in her report how arms delivered by the USA to the Indonesian army play a crucial role in the human rights violations she describes in her report.

Does the official acceptance of her report render "the USA" hypocritical? Again, I find it clearer to talk about specific officials here. Take President Bush, for example, who caused thousands of people to be tortured horribly: at Abu Ghraib, and Guantánamo Bay, and also—much worse—at many "black sites" at unknown locations and through "extraordinary renditions" to "friendly" countries like Syria, Yemen, Jordan, and Egypt. In a statement that he issued in 2004 on the UN International Day in Support of the Victims of Torture, he said:

The United States reaffirms its commitment to the worldwide elimination of torture.... The victims often feel forgotten, but we will not forget them. America supports

41

accountability and treatment centers for torture victims.... We stand with the victims to seek their healing and recovery, and urge all nations to join us in these efforts to restore the dignity of every person affected by torture.

(June 26, 2004; available at www.america.gov/st/
washfile-english/2004/June/20040628140800LShsa
N0.3632013.html)

This strikes me as a good case of hypocrisy insofar as Bush presented himself as personally endorsing the worldwide elimination of torture and accountability with respect to torture, as well as treatment centers, healing, recovery, and restoration of dignity for torture victims, even while he was also authorizing torture, working hard to ensure that there would be no accountability with regard to the torture he was deliberately causing and authorizing, and no treatment centers, no healing, no recovery, and no restoration of dignity for the many (often innocent) victims of such torture.

Your third case again raises interesting difficulties. The judge may be applying the law without endorsing it, or may be endorsing it as a useful instrument of public order without endorsing it as generating genuine moral duties. To illustrate the first case, take a law against homosexuality. The judge believes this law to be unjust and works to change it to the extent he can. He is also a practicing homosexual. But his legal philosophy is such that he feels himself bound to apply the law as it is. In this case, the judge is not hypocritical. He is not publicly endorsing the normative position he is personally contravening. To illustrate the second case, take a law against possession of heroin. The judge thinks this is a good law because most citizens would not be able to handle heroin properly, and it is just not feasible to exempt the few who can. But our judge also believes that this law does not impose a genuine moral duty, certainly not on those few who can handle heroin properly. Believing himself to be among this number, he tries heroin. He is not a hypocrite, because he does not endorse the position that it is always wrong to break this law—only the position that it is permissible to punish legally those who break it.

"Recently, an American general was criticized for airing his personal belief that homosexuality is immoral. If we hold certain beliefs sincerely, but know that said beliefs may offend other people, are we obliged to be quiet about them? I can understand why many people found the general's attitude reprehensible; at the same time, however, criticizing him for that attitude makes about as much sense to me as getting upset over his liking vanilla ice cream. Can we rightly blame people for the preferences they happen to have?"

Roger Crisp:

There's an important difference between airing one's beliefs or preferences and merely possessing them. Many feel that criticizing people for their beliefs is unfair, since beliefs aren't voluntary and one can be held responsible only for what's voluntary. But some philosophers doubt this (see, for example, the philosopher Robert M. Adams's wonderful paper "Involuntary Sins"). Imagine someone whose beliefs about homosexuality are unusually vicious—perhaps they think gays should be tortured. Even if we think this person's beliefs are involuntary, we'll probably be tempted to criticize them. It may be, of course, that this kind of criticism is of a different kind from that we use in the case of voluntary action.

But this general didn't just hold these beliefs. He uttered them, and that is something that he can be held responsible for in the ordinary sense. Here I suspect people might want to criticize him from two angles. First, it might be thought that he was violating some principle of professional ethics. He was speaking as a member of the US Army, and shouldn't have said anything that was against US Army policy or might plausibly be seen as bringing the Army into disrepute. Second, his comment raises questions about the limits of freedom of speech, most famously discussed in J. S. Mill's *On Liberty*. What one thinks about such limits is going to depend on one's general moral view. But something like Mill's view is quite common: that speech can be criticized if it is potentially harmful to others. Given that people often attack or discriminate against gays, speech that encourages such action should be criticized.

DEATH

" *If by my death I could save another's life (like falling on a grenade), do I have a moral obligation to do so? Are there circumstances when this might or might not be true? Are there schools of philosophy or specific works that address this question?* "

Miranda Fricker:

One can perhaps imagine circumstances in which it made ethical sense that someone should sacrifice their own life for that of another person. For instance, one might sacrifice oneself to save one's child. We might feel such an act is an especially good act, one that goes above and beyond the call of duty (a "supererogatory" act). But the idea that one might have an *obligation* to sacrifice one's own life for another is a much stronger idea.

I doubt there is anything much in Kant's moral philosophy—a moral theory that organizes all acts of moral worth as done out of a motive of duty—to entail the duty to sacrifice one's own life for that of another, but a moral theory that surely does speak to this idea is consequentialism. Basic forms of consequentialism say that the rightness or wrongness of an action consists exclusively in the goodness or badness of its consequences—the motive is not independently relevant. Now this tends to generate a standing obligation to maximize the good (whether the good turns out to be human happiness, preference satisfaction, minimization of pain, etc.), and that standing obligation would entail a moral obligation to sacrifice one's own life *whenever* doing so would cause less unhappiness/preference frustration/human pain/etc. than not doing so.

Your question thereby throws up two of the cardinal problems with what is called "act" consequentialism, which requires us to maximize good consequences with each action we do. First, it is too demanding: the standing obligation to maximize the good on every occasion of action is too burdensome, and doesn't leave enough room in life for other values. Second, we're not generally in a position to judge which of two prospective actions that present themselves (such as throwing oneself on the grenade or not) is the better maximizing strategy. Both of these criticisms inspire what is often called "rule consequentialism": the form of consequentialism that says our standing moral obligation is not to maximize the good with every action, but rather to adhere to a set of rules or practices which, taken overall, constitute the best collective maximizing strategy.

"*I am a student at Lafayette College, and last weekend we celebrated the Marquis de Lafayette's 250th birthday.*

46

Is such a celebration valuable to the Marquis himself, even when he is dead?"

Amy Kind:

You raise an interesting question, one that philosophers have worried about. Assuming that there's no afterlife, and that once you're dead you're dead, how can something that happens after your death harm you or benefit you? After all, you're not around to experience it.

This presupposes, however, an experiential account of harms and benefits. And we might think that there can be harms and benefits that exist outside of our experiences. Suppose that your best friend secretly hates you and is talking about you behind your back, although she's perfectly pleasant to you and so her behavior has no effect on your experience. Would you mind? Insofar as you *would* mind, and I certainly would, then you probably think that harms can occur outside of experience. And so, even though the Marquis no longer has any experiences, maybe he can still be harmed or benefited by things that occur.

Then again, your institution may not even have any pretense of having a celebration that's for the value of the Marquis himself. It could have value for the college community instead: team building, instilling institutional pride, giving everyone a day off from classes, etc. Think of wakes or memorial services. In many ways, these events are really for the living. They allow survivors to experience catharsis, to come together after a loss and find comfort in other people, etc., etc. So even if your celebration has no value for your college's namesake, that's not to say it has no value.

Peter S. Fosl:

My hometown is Bethlehem, PA, and I spent plenty of time around Lafayette and downtown Easton growing up, so I had to respond to this. I hope things are well there with you.

I agree with my colleague Amy Kind that people can be harmed or benefited even if they're unaware of it. If that's so, perhaps in a sense even the dead can be harmed or benefited. A colleague of mine used to speak of harm in terms not of experience but of interests, and we might call one of the kinds of interests people have "narrative interest"—that is, an interest in the story of their life. Most of us, I think, have an interest in our reputations. Some of us maintain an interest in producing a reputation that endures after we've died. Indeed, the narrative of our life in a sense defines who we are. So, who the Marquis was is determined today in part by the physical artifacts and remains related to him but also, importantly, by the narrative of his life. If someone were to ask, "Who was the Marquis de Lafayette?" The answer is likely to be informed by the current story of his life. And damaging the Marquis's life story would, therefore, damage who he now is, an historical personage.

Concern for one's narrative interests might not be terribly admirable, a product of vanity and excessive pride or ambition. On the other hand, an interest in an enduring reputation might serve moral virtue to the extent that it, say, sustains a family name or enhances the reputation of a good institution (perhaps a college or a nation) to which one has been connected. So, celebrating the Marquis's memory not only in a strange way benefits him. It also benefits France, the United States, your college, and his descendants, etc. (But, of course, harm and benefit aren't exactly the terms you used. As to whether or not the celebration is "valuable" to him, I'd have to say that strictly speaking it's not.)

In any case, keep this in mind: regardless of whether it benefits the Marquis to celebrate him, it's a good thing for us to remember past people who have made valuable contributions to our present condition. In fact, I might go so far as to say that the cultivation of an historical memory of this sort is a key ingredient of civilization, and a very good thing for us. The dead often present useful role models, serve as better reminders of important principles and values than abstract ideas, and the dead inspire and motivate us. Remembering them contributes to a sense of self-worth and identity.

Go Leopards!

"*Is all morality based on the belief that death is a bad thing? If we believed that death was desirable, for whatever reason, would morality break down, or at least be turned upside down?"*

Jyl Gentzler:

In Plato's dialogue *Phaedo*, Socrates explains to his friends why, in the face of his imminent execution, he is in a good mood. His whole life, he reports, has been a preparation for death (64a–b): after he dies, his soul will be separated from his body, and he will finally be able to attain the only thing of genuine value— knowledge of the forms (65b–e, 66b–67b, 69a–b). If Socrates is right, Cebes rightly asks, why shouldn't we all commit suicide? (61b). Because, Socrates rather lamely responds, we are the property of the gods, and they should decide when we die (62b–c). Without such a view about the property rights of the gods, Cebes' question is difficult for a person like the Socrates of the *Phaedo* to answer. We might think that suicide would be wrong because in death we are unable to meet our responsibilities to others, but what sense can one make of these responsibilities if they, too, would be better off dead?

Despite what Socrates suggests about the extraordinary virtues of philosophers who are convinced by his doctrine, it seems to me that if it really were true, as the questioner suggests, that death was more desirable than life, then our whole moral system would be out of whack. Sure, the philosopher who is aiming for death would be bold in battle since he wouldn't fear death. But what could possibly motivate him to fight for the lives of his fellow citizens, if, in fact, death would be a blessing to them? Wouldn't he be benefitting his enemies by killing them? And what sense could one make of the virtue of justice, if there were no genuine goods in this life to distribute more or less fairly?

I think, though, that despite Socrates' many arguments for the immortality of the soul and the promise of knowledge of the forms in the afterlife, we have no good reason to believe that (except in cases of terrible suffering) death is anything other than a loss, one of the greatest losses one can suffer, and that for this reason, our moral codes rightly demand that we work hard to protect human life.

SUICIDE

"What strikes me as the most terrible effect of suicide is the great pain that those left behind often experience. But does this mean that we are literally obligated to stay alive for the sake of other people?"

Thomas Pogge:

What about other decisions you face? Does it strike you as strange that anyone should ultimately have any reason to *act* other than in the service of his own happiness? If so, you are challenging all moral obligations; and you would then find it just as strange that anyone should be "literally obligated" to refrain from rape and murder.

I assume that this is not your view—that you accept some obligations toward others and are willing to take their interests into account, alongside your own, when deciding how to act. But if this is the way you think about your ordinary decisions, then why should the decision about suicide be special? If your mother's feelings are a reason for you to call her on her birthday, then why are they not also a reason to refrain from committing suicide?

The illusion that we have no obligation to consider others' interests when contemplating suicide may arise from two sources. First, many jurisdictions forbid committing suicide and assisting someone else commit suicide. This may strike us as exceeding society's legitimate authority. A society does not own its citizens, and when a fully competent citizen wants to die, and perhaps wants a friend's help with this, then society should not stand in the way. We may reject the intrusion of society and its law in our decision about suicide, and we may further conclude that we have no moral obligation to comply with such an unjust law. From this we may then falsely infer that we have no moral obligations toward others in this matter.

(An analogous mistake is common with regard to freedom of speech. We strongly reject the idea that society's law may constrain what we may say or write. But on reflection we realize, nonetheless, that we sometimes say things that we morally ought not to have said—even if saying them was legal and rightly so. With regard to speech, then, the law ought not forbid all that it is morally wrong to express. This case shows what is not at first obvious: the fact that some action ought to be legally permitted is compatible with this action's being morally wrong. In some cases, citizens ought to have a legal right to do the morally wrong thing. Suicide may be one such case.)

The other source of the illusion is the very great pain that people contemplating suicide are typically experiencing. In comparison to this pain, the interests of others may pale to insignificance, especially for the person longing to die. To correct for this illusion, we can imagine an unusual case: a guy who is a bit bored with life, whose car mirror was damaged, and who is fighting the third pimple on his chin in a single month. He is not especially eager to live or to die, but feels mildly inclined to do himself in. When so little is at stake for him, it is easier to appreciate that the interests of others may be strong enough to tip the scales. If his parents, siblings, spouse, and children would all be totally devastated by his suicide, surely he ought to pull himself together, get that mirror repaired, fight the new pimple with aftershave, and find something exciting to do with his family. It would be wrong for him to let his very slight preference outweigh the devastating effects his suicide would have on others.

This case suggests what I think is the right answer to your query. In this matter, as in all others, we have a moral obligation to take the interests of others into account. This does not mean that we have a general obligation to stay alive for their sake. In some cases the interests of others really do pale to insignificance in comparison to one's own, and in such cases suicide is permissible, perhaps after one has done what one can do to ease the pain of those left behind. Yet in other cases, like that of the preceding paragraph, one does have a moral obligation to stay alive for the sake of others.

> " *Could someone ever be responsible for another's suicide? I don't mean to include cases in which, for example, someone gives a weapon to an unstable person. The person I have in mind causes severe emotional distress to another person who ultimately kills himself.* "

Kalynne Pudner:

Yes, though I wouldn't want to have to adjudicate responsibility in a particular case.

Here's the philosophical principle I've got in mind: If person A provides sufficient motivation for person B to commit an act, then A might be responsible for B's act. If A intended to provide sufficient motivation, intending that B commit the act, then I can't imagine A's *not* being responsible. And if B would not have committed the act but for A's motivating actions—in other words, if whatever A did was also necessary to B's committing the act—and A knew this, then A would definitely be responsible.

The problem with applying this general principle to suicides is that what counted as sufficient and necessary motivational conditions for a particular suicide are almost never known for certain. Most suicide victims (as I understand it) are assumed not to be in full rational control of their actions; e.g., there is mental illness involved. If suicide is an irrational act, then assigning responsibility will be a formidably difficult, if not moot, task.

In the case you describe, if the person causing severe emotional distress intended to push the victim to suicide, and the victim would not have committed suicide but for the infliction of the severe emotional distress, then yes, s/he is responsible. If the person causing the distress never intended to push the victim to suicide, but knew (or should reasonably have known) that it might, and the victim would not have committed suicide but for the distress, then I'd say yes again. But if the victim would have committed suicide anyway, then the person causing the distress would not be responsible, even if s/he intended to do it (though some might disagree with me here). If the suicide has been successful, could we ever know what role the emotional distress actually played?

This isn't a precise illustration, but I think it might be relevant to sorting out the issue: Depressed patients given anti-depressants show a significant rate of suicide, so there's been some concern that anti-depressants are responsible for patients' committing suicide. But one of the more notable symptoms of depression is extreme lethargy. So these patients may have been intending suicide all along, but they didn't have the energy to carry it out until the anti-depressant alleviated the lethargy. In logical terms, the anti-depressant didn't provide a sufficient condition for the suicide, but rather a necessary one. Normally providing a necessary condition doesn't assign responsibility unless it was done with the intent of providing a necessary condition. The doctors who prescribed anti-depressants for these patients never intended to provide the necessary energy for the patient to go through with a previously-planned suicide, so they wouldn't be responsible.

"Why is suicide illegal? Should it be illegal?"

Thomas Pogge:

Suicide has been outlawed in different societies and epochs for all sorts of different reasons. These reasons fall broadly into three categories: to enforce religious commands, to protect persons from themselves, and to protect persons other than the would-be suicide. Are these *good* reasons to outlaw suicide?

Reasons in the first category are not acceptable in modern democratic societies (and, in the USA, violate the First-Amendment separation of church and state).

Those in the majority must not impose their religion on their fellow citizens.

Reasons in the second category—so-called paternalistic reasons—can be plausible. It is a good thing that the police can stop the attempted suicide of a young man who is in despair after his lover broke up with him. Chances are he'll get over it and fall in love again, even if this now seems inconceivable to him. But what if, a year or two later, the man still judges his life not worth living and wants to die? Who are we to overrule his judgment in this matter? We may perhaps legally require would-be suicides to receive competent information from relevant experts (doctors, psychologists, etc.) and from others who have gone through a crisis similar to theirs. But when someone has done this, and still wants to die, we should not force him to stay alive "for his own sake." (Note that, in practice, modern democratic societies do not apply such coercion even though they do make suicide illegal. And criminal punishments for attempted suicide are exceedingly rare.)

Reasons in the third category invoke the interests of those who depend on the would-be suicide. This does not include the interests of society or other larger groups. A person is free to withdraw from these groups (to quit her job, to leave her religious group, to emigrate), and this shows that they have no right to her continued contributions. The same point would seem to hold, to a lesser extent, for a spouse: The fact that a person is free to have a divorce shows that her spouse has no right to her continued partnership. The interests of a dependent child, however, support a much stronger claim. To be sure, society must find a way to meet the needs of the child if its parent dies. But the loss of a parent, especially through suicide, is often a devastating loss for a child even if society meets its obligation well (something that, in the real world, is often not the case).

In conclusion, I think there are sufficiently strong reasons in the second and third categories for outlawing not all suicides, but some, in a way designed to discourage and to express disapproval. These reasons are strongest with respect to persons with dependent children who experience a kind of crisis that tends to be temporary. These reasons may justify restraining competent people for brief periods. And they may justify forcing competent persons to receive balanced information and counseling relating to their crisis and to the potential impact of their decision on their dependent children.

"My son just committed suicide, at age 18, after battling schizophrenia for eleven years. He had a terrible time with the panic attacks, the hallucinations, and the debilitating drugs. I am distraught and heartbroken, and miss him terribly, but I also see his decision as a positive one, given the circumstances. Am I morally wrong if I can understand why my son took his own life, and maybe even believe that he made the right decision?"

Allen Stairs:

Let me begin by saying that I'm sorry for your loss. This must be terribly hard. And your sense of guilt is understandable. It's hard to think the thought that one's child may have done the best thing in taking his own life. But as you point out, this thought doesn't come from lack of care or lack of grief, but from the very opposite: from deep caring and empathy born of intimate knowledge of your son's situation.

There are some well-known theological and philosophical arguments intended to show that suicide is always wrong. Immanuel Kant offered one that strikes many readers—it certainly strikes me this way—as bordering on sophistry; I won't try to reconstruct it here, and won't recommend it as anything you need consider. Theological arguments against suicide often rest on dubious claims about the divine will and the way in which taking one's own life supposedly usurps God's prerogative to decide when we die, arguments that might well make a believer in a loving and merciful God shudder. But the sense of many reflective people is that these abstract arguments are beside the point in evaluating the actions of someone whose life promises only continued misery.

Of course, none of this is meant to suggest that we should have a casual attitude toward suicide, nor that suicide is always rational or right. But blanket prohibitions that take no account of real people's pain and prospects can't be justified and have the side-effect of making those left behind feel needlessly guilty for empathizing with the person who took his life.

Philosophers are by temperament people who tend not to care too much about what "society" thinks if society's views seem ill-founded. Society is in no position to pass judgment on the very personal details of your son's life and death. Your words are the words of a loving parent; whatever some people may think, you aren't wrong for feeling as you do.

Oliver Leaman:

I don't think you are wrong to have such a belief, and we can all think of situations in which people might come to the reasonable conclusion that death was preferable to life. I would not be overly concerned at feelings of guilt, because we often feel guilt for things over which we have no control at all. It is not as though in a fit of sudden despair when you were not available to be with him he carried out this act. He thought about it over some time, calmly considered the various options and likely eventualities, no doubt including your feelings in the matter and the effect his action would have on you, and came to a certain conclusion. I think we have to respect the decisions of our children, especially when they veer away from where we would like them to go, and not feel guilt as a result of them.

On the other hand, in the case of someone on medication and with mental health problems one is always worried about how far autonomy is at issue. Did he really have the ability to make a calm and measured decision, or was his thinking unbalanced by a particular combination of drugs, or indeed their absence? In that case one might be worried about whether prompt intervention of some kind might have brought about a different conclusion. Then guilt would be appropriate. From the account you provide, though, this is not the situation, and I am sure you would understand the nature of what was taking place much better than anyone else. There is no reason why suicide need not be a brave and defiant act, and you should have no compunction at so describing it.

THE PUBLIC

MEDICINE

"*Imagine I am a scientist working for a pharmaceutical company, and I spend 25 years working on a drug that will cure a disease. I patent my work, but the patent only lasts for 8 years. In that time, the pharmaceutical company sells the drug at a high price but uses most of its profits to fund more research. After 8 years, anyone can replicate my drug. Why should I allow generic brands, during those 8 years, to make my drug? I know many more people would have access to it if I did, but my work is not only funding more research but is something I invested a great portion of my life in. Is there a good argument for allowing generic drugs in that case?*"*

Thomas Pogge:

Your reasoning appeals to a false dichotomy. You assume that *either* we give monopoly pricing powers to inventors and thereby effectively deny access to recent drugs to poor patients, *or* we allow generic companies to compete and thereby effectively deprive inventors of their rewards and of funds for new research ventures. But there are further options.

One such option would be to allow generic companies to compete immediately (thereby reducing the price of a new medicine to near the marginal cost of production) and then to reward inventors in another way, for example with a reward (out of public funds) proportioned to the impact of their invention on the global disease burden. All patients would benefit from much cheaper access to recent drugs, and taxpayers would pay a little more. Millions of lives would be saved through this innovation—not merely because poor patients would get access to cutting-edge drugs, but also because biotech and pharmaceutical companies would gain an incentive to research remedies for the diseases that predominantly affect the poor and an incentive also to work toward the optimal deployment of such remedies once they exist.

So, while I agree with you that inventors should be rewarded—for fairness to them and also for encouraging and enabling new research ventures—I don't see how this needs to come (as it now does) at the expense of poor patients.

"An eleven-year-old child lies on the operating table, dying from an accident. He asks his doctor if he is going

to die. If the doctor thinks he will, should he tell the child?"

Miriam Solomon:

The salient feature of this question is that the dying person is an eleven-year-old child, rather than an adult. Our sympathy is aroused and we wish to protect the child from pain, especially the pain of knowing that s/he is about to die. But first, I think it is important to ask the question: if the dying person were an adult, would it be appropriate to lie about the prognosis? And I think the answer is "No, the adult has a right to be told the truth about their prognosis." So if an adult has that right, why not a child?

Some would say that a child couldn't handle such information. But I think that depends on the child—and many eleven-year-olds might be able to handle the information as well as adults, and might use it to do certain important things, such as make final statements or requests. The work of anthropologist Myra Bluebond-Langner in *The Private Worlds of Dying Children* (Princeton University Press, 1978) on dying children shows that children often handle the topic of their own death as maturely as (or more maturely than) adults do.

"Is it ethical for surgeons to use economic considerations when setting their fees? For example, is it ethical for a surgeon who is known to have better results for a

certain operation to charge more than a surgeon who has worse results? Likewise, is it ethical for a surgeon who has a skill that is scarce in a particular region to charge exorbitant fees for that skill simply because most patients could not afford to travel to another region to attend another surgeon?"

Peter S. Fosl:

This is a fascinating question because medical care is not a commodity like many others, such as televisions or ice cream. It is a service related to the most profound of human needs. For that reason, I answer your first question with a "no"—but with qualification. It really depends upon what you mean by "economic considerations." I think it would be wrong to use simple supply and demand considerations where the supplier (the surgeon) charged the highest price the market will bear. Why? Because higher prices will exclude those with less money from the service, and I don't think it is morally defensible to distribute essential medical services on the basis of wealth. Moreover, people suffering from illness are not in a position to bargain for fees with medical providers in the absence of coercion. (Think of how little a surgeon would charge if he or she were at risk of dying if a prospective patient decided to seek care elsewhere!) For this reason, I find the American medical system on the whole to be morally deficient. A fairer and more equitable system of distributing medical services must be found than market rationing. On the other hand, "economic considerations" might also mean considerations of the financial needs of patients. Setting a sliding scale or making other provisions to deliver healthcare to the financially needy would be permissible and, really, morally virtuous.

Thomas Pogge:

It may also matter what sort of operation we are talking about. If this is cosmetic surgery—say, beautifying belly buttons—then the service does seem quite similar to other commodities, such as face cream, and the reasons against the surgeon's charging what she will seem quite weak.

As we move to the other end of the spectrum to operations that are a matter of life and death, Peter Fosl's points become ever more compelling. Such operations should not be rationed on the basis of wealth: A medically important operation that is routinely available to the wealthy should also be available, in roughly the same quality, to the poor. Call this the *medical equity principle* (MEP).

Now, it does not follow from the MEP that it is unethical for the best surgeons to charge more. Societies that have organized themselves around the MEP need to have enough high-quality doctors to take care of the medical needs of all. To attract people into the profession of surgeon, and to entice them to become really good surgeons, such an MEP society may arrange itself so that the income of surgeons reflects their level of skill. Why shouldn't a top surgeon who lives in an MEP society take the high remuneration available to her just as other surgeons with her outstanding skills are also doing in this society?

In our society, which is obviously not organized around the MEP, billions are spent on small improvements and extensions of the lives of the affluent even while poor uninsured Americans lack access to important medical services and millions of child deaths abroad could be avoided each year at the cost of a few US dollars per case. These grotesque violations of the MEP are a very grave injustice, in my view. An important aspect of your questions is, then, how one ought to behave in a context of grave injustice. By demanding from every patient what the market will bear for a medically important operation, a highly skilled surgeon would be both contributing to and taking advantage of a grave injustice: She would be contributing to the unjust segregation of patients by wealth, and she would be taking advantage of the fact that the social context is one in which patients must bid for top-flight medical treatment. Plausibly, what such a surgeon should do is earn her living by charging the affluent what the market will bear, and then give equally good service to poor people for what they can comfortably afford (which may sometimes be $0).

Last point. It is not only top surgeons who, in an unjust social context, have responsibilities to shield people from grievous effects of injustice. Affluent citizens should understand that, if our society were just and thus in reasonable compliance with the MEP, then people like themselves would have lower net incomes (as more of the social product would be spent on ensuring that all have access to important medical care). Understanding this, affluent citizens should not just pocket the fruits of injustice, but should spend some of their wealth on supporting political reforms or on protecting the victims of injustice. We all should help put access to medical care on the political agenda and elect politicians who are firmly committed to moving this country and the world closer to compliance with the MEP.

"Should people who make health-damaging choices like smoking, drinking, abusing drugs, and overeating be denied organ transplants if their organs fail as a result of these choices?"

Nicholas D. Smith:

I don't see why. If there is reason to think that these bad choices would continue in such a way as to make the transplant likely to fail, then I can see having them be a factor. But if a patient needs a transplant, then it does not seem to me to be up to the medical profession to deny that transplant on some moralistic ground.

Consider two cases, in which each patient needs a kidney transplant. In one case (A), we have good reason to believe that the patient needs the transplant because of drug abuse earlier in his life. (Let's not complicate the issue further by going into how likely we think it is that the person might return to drug abuse if the transplant is done successfully.) In the other case (B), we see no such evidence, but we also know that the person has been guilty several times in his life of physically or sexually abusing members of his family in numerous ways. Imagine finally that these are the only plausible candidates for this transplant—the kidney will spoil and be useless to anyone if the transplant is not made in the next day. Should it be a medical decision to withhold the transplant from either of these individuals because of what we know about them?

The reason I give these cases is because I think that there may be any number of factors that might incline us to favor one candidate over another for a transplant. Maybe A is also a really funny person who is charming to be with and B is a total grouch liked by very few people. Should that matter? I can sympathize with those who feel the pull of such considerations, but I really think it would be a very bad idea to have doctors or medical staff making medical decisions based on such factors.

Medical teams do have criteria they apply to these decisions, and perhaps the self-inflicted nature of some medical conditions should count as a kind of "tie-breaker" in otherwise similar cases. But bringing in more such considerations seems to me to be an extremely risky business, and judgments about the relevance of these considerations are not appropriately made by medical professionals.

BUSINESS

"*Do very large corporations have a duty to be ethical and to involve themselves in charity? Is the duty of a pharmaceutical company that makes life-saving drugs any greater than the duty of a company that produces frivolous things, like sparkly party hats?*"

Matthew Silverstein:

This is an interesting question. Actually, I think you're asking two different questions here: (1) Do corporations have a duty to behave in an ethical manner, and (2) Does ethical behavior necessarily involve charity?

The answer to the first question is certainly that corporations *do* have a duty to behave ethically. They have duties, for instance, not to include false or misleading statements in their advertisements, not to use harmful chemicals in their products (whether these products are life-saving drugs or sparkly party hats), not to contaminate the water supply, and so forth. The second question is more difficult. After all, ethical theorists disagree about whether and to what extent *individuals* have a positive duty to give to charity (or, more generally, to be beneficent). And even if you're convinced that individuals *do* have such a duty, that hardly settles the question of whether corporations have one as well.

I tend to favor consequentialist moral theories. A consequentialist might argue that the best overall consequences would come about if corporations concentrated all of their energy solely on their business and left the charity to the owners or shareholders who receive the profits of this business. This sort of focus on business would insure that the profits available for donations to charity are as large as possible. On the other hand, if the CEO of a corporation has sufficient reason to believe that the shareholders will not donate a significant share of the profits to charity, then perhaps he or she has an obligation to order donations from the corporation itself. But this raises a host of ethical questions concerning the obligations executives have regarding shareholders.

"*One of my favorite rap artists used to be a drug dealer and a pimp. He is not apologetic, and regularly brags about it. If I buy his albums, am I supporting drug dealing and pimping?*"

Allen Stairs:

Perhaps, as you'd expect, it depends on what we mean.

One scenario: the artist used the profits from his musical career to underwrite drug dealing and prostitution. In that case, you're supporting drug dealing and pimping at least in the sense that you're helping to provide the cash that keeps it running.

Another scenario: the artist isn't dealing drugs and pimping, but his fame and the reach of his CD sales help him encourage others to do what he used to do. In that case, your money is still supporting criminal activities, though quite a bit less directly.

I'm guessing the most likely scenario is this. As far as you know, he isn't still carrying on any criminal enterprises. As far as you know, he probably does mean to glorify those things, and as far as you know, he probably does have at least some marginal success in encouraging others to do the things he used to do. In other words, even if he's no longer an active criminal, there's something unsavory here, and the more successful he is financially, the more that's so. But I'm also guessing that you just like his music and aren't interested in promoting drugs or pimping. Where does that leave you?

Nowhere particularly clear. On the one hand, most of us spend money that supports businesses whose practices may be undesirable even if not criminal, and many of us even know some specific cases. Corporation X sells a product I want, but contributes to causes I deplore, or engages in labor or environmental or business practices that I oppose. These days, purity isn't easy to come by. A few years ago, for better or worse, the town council where I live declared itself a "nuclear free zone," meaning that they wouldn't do business with any company that had a stake in the nuclear industry. Turned out this was almost impossible to pull off without tying themselves in knots.

I may buy something from a company whose practices I don't like. But when I do, I may be doing it with my nose held, so to speak—in spite of what I don't like about them. I'm not vicariously indulging in their vices. That's where the music case seems a little different. The connections between the artist, the message, and what the consumer expresses by supporting the artist seem tighter and more intimate than the connections in a general company–consumer case. If someone spouts whole-heartedly misogynist lyrics, the excuse that I'm buying their records just because I like the music is a bit malodorous. Hiving off the obnoxious content from everything else and putting it in a box might be possible, but I have a feeling I'd suspect myself of bad faith.

Here's an interesting case. Suppose that I stumbled across some artist whose language I didn't even speak. I start buying his CDs, and then a friend who knows the language points out that what he's singing amounts to Nazi propaganda. I don't think I'd feel good about where my money went, and I don't think I'd want to put any more in the artist's coffers.

So: buying this artist's CDs isn't the worst thing you could do. But it doesn't seem entirely innocent, either. And the less incidental the glorification of crime is to the music, the harder it is to claim that you've stayed on the unsullied side.

"Let's say I like, but don't need, a piece of software. After shopping around, I find that the lowest price is way, way above what I'm willing to pay for it, and so I decide not to buy it. Then I find an opportunity to download it from the Internet for free. If I download it and use the software, I'll be breaking the law. But will I have done something morally wrong? I'm not depriving the software developer of any revenue, as I wouldn't consider buying the software at retail price."

Saul Traiger:

Let's begin by asking where the copy of the software on the Internet came from. Presumably someone purchased a licensed copy. Typically, commercial software licenses limit further reproduction and distribution. So the original purchaser agreed to the conditions of the license, and consummated that agreement when installing the software. More directly: The purchaser promised not to further distribute it.

So you've come across this software on the Internet, and you know that its availability is the consequence of someone's broken promise. You did not make the promise, but you are knowingly benefiting from some-one else's moral failure. Compare the situation to buy-ing a used car from someone who stole it, when you know the car is stolen. You may know, as well, that the original owner is fully covered by insurance, and will not suffer any financial loss. But is it morally OK to buy such a car? Does it matter that you wouldn't have pur-chased the car from another source because you aren't willing to pay the market rate?

SPORTS AND GAMES

"*Although there is obviously a distinction between play-ing a game with simulated violence and actually commit-ting acts of violence, is it immoral to enjoy violent games? Is enjoyment of simulated violence wrong, and, if so, where do we draw the line? Is chess immoral, since the point is to crush your opponent's army? How does the accuracy of simulation affect the morality of a violent game?*"

Louise Antony:

I suspect that when people think it's immoral for some-one to enjoy a violent video game, they are presuming that they know the answer to what is in fact an empirical question: Do the attitudes and appetites that the gamer is indulging during play carry over to real life? Does the bloodlust of the gamer cause real bloodlust? Will playing such games render the gamer less sensitive to real violence? My experience suggests that the gamer's attitudes do not carry over to real life. I like to play violent video games, but I can only remember one instance in my whole life in which I actually hit someone (my son, and I sorely regret it), and I'm still revolted by photos or descriptions of torture and war. I'm not the only one like this: If I were, then either violent movies would be a lot less popular, or there would be a lot more murderous rampaging going on than there is. I suspect that for the games and movies to be fun, it's really important that the players and the audiences know that it's all pretend.

But I reiterate: This is really an empirical question. And it turns out to be hard to answer. To test it, you need to have a good measure of what someone's attitudes are before and after playing the game (or watching the movie). But how do you get such a measure? Many studies have subjects fill out questionnaires, but it's not known what such responses really indicate. Even if the "aggression" responses increase (and sometimes they do not), it's unclear how long-lasted or serious such responses are. It's also not known exactly what features of the games and movies are producing the effect—perhaps the effect is the result of any high excitement.

I think the same question can and should be asked about pornography. It is possible, as some feminists contend, that indulging sexual responses to images of women being degraded or dehumanized carries over to one's attitudes toward real women. But this is an empirical question, and I think it's just as likely that people's sexual responses to various images depend on their believing that the images are pretend. As feminists have taken pains to emphasize, it is emphatically one thing for women to fantasize about being raped, and another thing for them to actually enjoy rape. If that's so, I don't see why a person who would never, ever consider raping a woman might not still enjoy fantasizing about raping a woman. (And for the record, I am a feminist.)

Thomas Pogge:

Louise says, "I don't see why a person who would never, ever consider raping a woman might not still enjoy fantasizing about raping a woman." I agree that this is possible. But this does not really answer the question whether there would be anything wrong with such fantasizing and such enjoyment. I think that this would be wrong *even if it did not lead to any kind of violent behavior toward actual women*. Why?

First, it would be wrong because the rape fantasizer could not know in advance what we assume to be true, namely that his fantasies would not cause him to be violent. He cannot know that, drunk or sober, exuberant or depressed, he'll never act out his fantasies when a "safe" opportunity presents itself. (To this one might respond that actual violence may be as easily triggered by *not* fantasizing about it as by fantasizing about it. Perhaps refraining from violent fantasies is as likely as its opposite to cause violence; by not fantasizing about violent rape, a man may be just as likely to make himself less safe as he is to make himself safer. From what I have read on the subject, I don't think this response has much chance of being true. But this is, of course, an empirical matter.)

Second, by allowing himself to enjoy rape fantasies and violent sex movies, a man disrupts his relationship with women and makes real friendship with women, let alone love, very difficult. For suppose you are a woman and you learn that a man you know hugely enjoys fantasies or movies that feature women being raped, degraded, beaten, mutilated, and so on. It would be difficult, if not impossible, for her to relate to such a person. (Louise, correct me if I'm wrong here.) Of course, the man might keep his hobby to himself and his male companions. But this poses a different problem for friendship in that a part of his life would then remain unsharable with her—a part she would deem important if she knew.

Third, there is the ethical task of self-development. We should lead our lives with an eye to being the best that we can be. To work out what the best life is for oneself takes some reflection, which itself is part of living well. People will reasonably come to different conclusions based on their talents, interests, and social environment. All this diversity notwithstanding, some people lead their lives better than others: ethically better. Now imagine a movie theater full of men screaming in delight as yet another unexpected violent sexual insult is visited on a young women tied to a bed. Even if this woman is actually a consenting and well-paid actress, is the enjoyment of these men part of the best that they can be?

Let me hasten to add in conclusion that I have not meant to say anything about what the law should be. I have focused narrowly on the question posed: Is it immoral to take—to make oneself into, or to rest content with being, someone who takes—pleasure in fictional violence? I think this is immoral for the reasons given. It is a serious ethical defect in a person even if it never manifests itself in his conduct.

"College sports are big business, and generate a tremendous amount of revenue. Should the players receive some share of that money?"

Richard Heck:

Before I begin, let me issue a quick reminder: Not all college sports are big business. Some of them are, to be sure: big-time college football, basketball, and the like. But college golf, tennis, swimming, and gymnastics don't generate much revenue, except perhaps at the most elite programs, and college sports don't generate much revenue at all at institutions like, say, MIT. So when I talk about college sports and "student athletes" below, I'm talking about only some college sports programs.

That said, I used to be a huge fan of college basketball. Now I hardly watch at all, and the reason the questioner mentions is perhaps the most significant. The rules governing (that is, prohibiting) the compensation of "student athletes" were put in place many years ago to protect the interests of such students. There was concern that a student might decide to go to school X rather than school Y, not because school X would better serve that student's long-term interests—which probably have little to do with sports—but rather because school X is offering certain kinds of financial incentives. That made a certain amount of sense.

But that was a *very* long time ago, when the term "student athlete" didn't need scare quotes. Now, the sports programs at many colleges and universities generate large sums of money. In most cases, that money is not even enough to cover the program's own expenses, let alone to make money for the colleges and universities themselves. But it is clear nonetheless that a lot of money is being made by someone. The "student athletes," however, are prohibited from receiving any of that money. Of course, "student athletes" do receive scholarships, but the real value of such compensation is trivial compared to what coaches, athletic directors, and other officials make. (Compare professional sports, where players typically make more money than the coaches and front office staff.) This is all the more worrying when so few "student athletes" graduate, and it's even more worrying when the graduation rate for black "student athletes" is far below that of white "student athletes" at most programs. (*Boston Globe* columnist Derrick Jackson publishes such statistics every year as regards football and basketball, and they are frightening.) The simple reason for this is that "student athletes" are admitted to colleges and universities absolutely all the time who have, *and are known to have,* absolutely no chance whatsoever of receiving a degree. Some of them, indeed, cannot even read. And they are given nothing like the support that would be required for them to succeed academically.

One might well reach the conclusion that "student athletes" are simply being exploited for four years and that the fruits of their labor are going to enrich the very people who claim to be protecting their interests.

"*As far as I know, the rules of soccer do not prohibit kicking the ball really hard at someone's face, if the person is in the way of the goal. But under normal circumstances, away from the soccer field, it's obviously wrong to go about blasting balls in people's faces. So how exactly does agreeing to the rules of a game remove normal moral constraints?"*

Douglas Burnham:

Boxing is an even more obvious example of a rule-governed sport that involves what would otherwise be immoral actions. The answer usually given lies in the notion of consent. By agreeing to be a part of the game, one consents to be subjected to such actions, and one is given the right to commit them in turn. There are some actions in sport that are not part of the rules, of course, and players have been subject to criminal prosecution for particularly violent tackles during a professional game.

However, it's not clear that this is the end of the story. For example, suppose it is the case that some forms of violence in sport feed a culture of acceptance, among viewers or participants, towards violence outside the sport. This is a question for empirical sociology or psychology, but the implications of the answer are ethical. In this case, consent *within* the sport may mean that one is consenting to more than one has the right to consent to: one is consenting on another's behalf, or one's consent takes away the possibility of the consent of another. In this case there may be good reasons for claiming that such violence is morally wrong. A similar argument is often employed concerning the morality of pornography.

INTERACTING WITH OTHERS

"*Does one good turn deserve another? Intuitively, when someone does something for me which I perceive as kind and selfless, I feel disposed to perform a similarly "kind" action for that person—more so than for some other person. But, if faced with the choice of selflessly helping person A, who once helped me, or person B, with whom I have no history, is there any moral reason why I should help person A? Why should the "good turn" which person A did me yesterday have a legitimate bearing on my decision today?*"

Miranda Fricker:

My own view is that, other things being equal, you do have a special reason to return a good turn, a reason that is lacking when you're considering performing a similarly good turn for a stranger. This is because ethical life is a mixture of reasons generated by a "partial" perspective (the perspective we take up when we are personally engaged with other people) and an "impartial" perspective (the perspective we take up when we are precisely not personally engaged, but are acting more like legislators of the good).

The place of partial reasons (what some philosophers call "agent-relative" reasons) remains controversial in philosophical ethics. There is ongoing debate about how far any moral reasons should take partial form, rather than a more impartial form that subsumes the values inherent in the partial perspective. So, for instance, one might think that the partial perspective can be honored by subsuming your reason to return a good turn under some general principle to the effect that "We should all return good turns done to us." Such a general principle expresses an impartial (or "agent-neutral") reason that attempts to subsume the partial reason. But others will not be satisfied with this. They might think that in converting partial reasons into impartial ones we lose the distinctive value of the partial reason, and end up constructing a moral system that is in unnecessary denial about the proper ethical place of partiality—of doing good things out of love, out of friendship, out of special personal concern, out of personal commitment, and so on. Ask yourself whether you think that someone's moral reason and motivation for helping their friend Amy properly takes the form "People should help their friends, and Amy is my friend," or whether the fundamental moral value of such loyalty is better expressed in the following irreducibly partial reason "Amy needs help."

Kant's moral philosophy is a classic expression of impartialism in ethics (see his *Groundwork for a*

Metaphysics of Morals). The philosopher Thomas Nagel explores these issues in his *The View From Nowhere.*

"Is it immoral to convince someone of some true proposition, by exposing that person to what you know to be a faulty argument? Suppose I tell my friend, "If it rains, the grass will be wet. The grass is wet, therefore, it rained." That's an invalid argument. But if it did rain, would it be immoral to use this invalid argument to convince her that it rained?"

Nicholas D. Smith:

I do think there is something wrong with using invalid arguments (at least ones that we know are invalid) to persuade people, both because it might habituate them to bad reasoning habits more generally, and because it is a kind of seduction. Consider: suppose you really believe that another person's best interests would be served by having sex with you (something you want with them). But you think you might not convince him or her just by being honest about your interest. So instead you seduce him or her in ways that are dishonest. Even if the other person's interests are ultimately served as a result of the seduction, the very fact of the seduction seems to me to be a clear violation of at least one of the person's interests—namely, not to be tricked, cheated, manipulated, or lied to. Using bad arguments that you know are bad is pure manipulation, like lying to another person. Bad medicine, even if it cures something!

Lorraine Besser-Jones:

Your question raises some fascinating issues. I think it will help to separate your question into two distinct concerns: (1) Is it immoral to use faulty reasoning to convince someone to believe something? (2) Is it immoral to place people in a situation in which they might believe something on the basis of faulty reasoning?

My first instinct is to say that situations involving (1) are likely to be immoral, whereas those involved in (2) are probably not. In cases of the first sort, cases in which you actively use poor reasoning to convince someone of something, there is a degree of deception at work. While most moral philosophers don't think that deception is always a bad thing, they nonetheless think it is bad absent special justification. We can imagine cases in which deception is harmless (as in your example) or even beneficial (for example, you might deceive your friend in order to get her to go to the doctor). But as a general rule, I think we do have a duty not to deceive people and that using faulty reasoning is a mode of deception.

However, I don't think that embracing this conclusion, and believing that it is immoral to use faulty reasoning to convince someone to believe something, commits one to believing that it is immoral to place people in a situation in which they might themselves engage in faulty reasoning. As a parent, I think I should avoid placing my children in such situations because I have a duty to help them learn and develop strong reasoning skills. But I don't think this is a duty that exists in the absence of this, or similar, relationships. Since in these cases you are not actively deceiving anyone, I don't think you are necessarily doing anything wrong. Of course we can imagine some cases in which you shouldn't place people in situations that might lead them to engage in faulty reasoning processes, but my sense is that what will make these cases wrong is something other than the mere fact that you have put them in a situation where they might engage in faulty reasoning processes.

"*There is a teacher in our school who often forgets if he gave us homework. The majority of the class takes advantage of this. I do not. Am I a fool for not wanting to use his weakness against him? If we continue to do the same lesson over and over like we're doing now, we will not learn anything new, but I will get a little less homework on my plate every night. Are the actions of the class immoral? Is it immoral to use someone's weakness against himself or herself for your own benefit?*"

Oliver Leaman:

Not necessarily, since using others' weakness is often a legitimate way of getting things we deserve. If someone in authority can be swayed to do what is right by playing on a weakness, there is no reason why we should not do so. The important issue here is whether the activity connected to the weakness is ethical or otherwise. If, as you think, it is hardly in your interest, or those of your colleagues, to repeat the same lesson a good deal, or to avoid homework which is after all useful in passing future examinations, then playing on the weakness is not to the pupils' long-term advantage. This is surely the nub of the issue, and you are not a fool for wanting to understand this material through homework and so to get in a position to move on to something new and perhaps more interesting.

"I believe in allowing other people to live out their respective journeys in life, even though this requires a lot of tolerance sometimes. How does one reconcile respecting another person's journey with the great harm that that person can do? In particular, I'm imagining someone who tries to force his beliefs on everyone else in an aggressive way. How does one respond to someone like that, morally speaking, while continuing to respect that person's journey of self-discovery?"

Jyl Gentzler:

When you say that you "believe in allowing other people to live out their respective journeys in life," do you make no exceptions? Do you think that it's a good idea to let anyone do anything that he or she sees fit? Liberals who are committed to tolerance often draw the line at actions that threaten great harm to others. After all, even liberals are committed to laws against murder, fraud, maiming, and the like, and most don't worry that their endorsement of such laws reveals a morally objectionable intolerance of people who are committed to different life plans from their own.

Your question raises interesting questions about when and why tolerance is a good thing. I think that many people are committed to tolerance because they believe that tolerance is the only attitude that is respectful of other people. But if a respectful attitude toward others is what people who are tolerant are attempting to achieve through their tolerance, then their commitment to tolerance cannot be absolute (i.e., exceptionless). My respect for human beings might in some circumstances commit me to being intolerant of other people's actions—namely, those harmful actions that themselves reveal a grossly disrespectful attitude toward other human beings.

"How great is our duty to protect other people from themselves? Does it extend from, say, removing the alcohol that an alcoholic has hidden away to telling a relative's children to eat their food politely, when the relative herself is indifferent to such matters? To what degree are we our brother's keeper?"

Peter S. Fosl:

As a parent, as an ever-older member of an extended family, and as a citizen of a somewhat democratic nation with a remarkably imprudent population, I struggle with this issue a lot. One way I think about this matter is first to make a distinction between (a) forcibly protecting people from themselves, (b) simply attempting to do so through persuasion, and (c) not acting at all. One general principle to keep in mind is that competent and independent people ought to be allowed maximal liberty, even to harm themselves, especially when significant pleasures are at stake. This helps us with clear cases.

For example, one has a duty to intervene forcibly to protect one's young children from themselves— say, by pulling their fingers away from an electrical socket. One's young children are neither competent nor independent.

There are, however, people who are competent but not independent. One arguably has a duty to protect one's grown children, when those children remain bound up with a parent–child relationship emotionally or financially. In such cases, however, so long as grown children remain competent, the duty becomes only one to attempt to persuade. Forcibly intervening with grown children is only a duty when the children have ceased to be competent—for example, through addiction, injury, or mental illness. And of course, in all cases, one arguably has no duty even to protect one's dependents if doing so places one's own well-being at serious risk.

When someone is incompetent but independent, one has an individual duty only when one is immediately presented with that person's attempt to harm himself or herself, and when the nature of the harm is extremely serious. So, for example, one does not have an individual duty to stop a stranger's child from smoking or an adult alcoholic from drinking. But one does have an obligation to stop a stranger's child from ingesting poison—so long, again, as doing so doesn't put oneself at risk. And one does have a duty to call the police if a drunk gets behind the wheel and tears off onto a crowded highway.

When people are competent and independent, one has no individual duty to protect them from themselves. But here things get tricky. As members of a shared society and as finite human beings, none of us are fully competent or fully independent. Limitations on knowledge, the coercive nature of various deprivations, etc., warrant a certain level of paternalism. And we are not only individual but social beings with not only individual but social or collective duties. So, the regulation of food and drugs is a social but not an individual duty. The obligations to prevent various forms of exploitation, to ensure safe workplaces, to require sufficient wages, to protect our environment from ourselves, and to make education, public safety, firefighting, and health care available, are social duties.

ENVIRONMENT

"Scientists, artists, poets, technocrats, philosophers, and others all respond to a phenomenon like global warming in different ways. What can philosophers bring to this serious planetary crisis?"

Thomas Pogge:

Philosophers can bring reflection on the responsibilities that contributors to global pollution have toward foreigners, future people, animals, and the rest of nature.

FOREIGNERS. Global warming is likely to cause severe harm to foreigners, from draughts in Africa to flooding in Bangladesh—especially to foreigners who are poor and vulnerable and who, for this reason, are themselves only very minimal contributors to global warming. Most of us shrug off the thought that we owe them anything. We think it's all right to pollute, or at least that our individual contribution is too small to matter. Is this an adequate response if millions die prematurely as a result of the pollution we together produce?

FUTURE PEOPLE. Global warming is likely to have devastating effects far in the future. In cost–benefit analyses, it is common to discount the interests of future people, typically by 3 percent per annum. This is thought plausible in analogy to how individuals discount future pains and pleasures—we are much more distraught when we face death tomorrow than when we face death in 40 years. But is the discounting of future people really plausible? Are deaths in 23 years only half as important, and deaths in 53 years one-fifth as important as deaths today? Is one human death today the moral equivalent of 500 deaths in 204 years, of 300,000 deaths in 414 years, and of 17 trillion human deaths in 1000 years?

ANIMALS AND THE REST OF NATURE. Global warming may wipe out many biological species and destroy places of natural beauty. Do these losses have any disvalue beyond the significance they have for us? Or are we human beings permitted to destroy all these beings and places so long as we are ready to do without them?

“ *I'm a print designer. Knowing how much waste and pollution is caused by my work, and given that I am concerned about having a healthy environment, is it unethical for me to continue my practice? If I stop, others will take my place. And although my work has a negative impact on the environment, it does serve people's needs and desires.* ”

Nicholas D. Smith:

Life is complicated, sure enough. My advice (for what it is worth) is for you to hang on to your job. Partly, this is precisely because your quitting your job (unless you have some other very clear option available to you in a "clean" occupation) won't make the least bit of difference to the project of ending waste and pollution, for the very reasons you gave: someone else will do it, and all you will have done is put yourself out of work.

Instead, why don't you consider—and urge your colleagues to consider—more environmentally friendly practices at work? For example, designs done on computers, rather than sketched on paper, create less paper waste. An out-of-date example, I'm sure, but I hope you get the point. Those with expertise in an industry are in the best position to find ways to cut waste and to come up with processes and products that are not so bad for the environment. Find these!

And where you can't find better solutions, consider "compensating" for it by, for example, planting trees at your place of work or in a local park. Quitting your job may seem very noble, but the reality is that you are likely to end up doing something just as bad, and if you stay, you may be able to make a positive difference.

"*I often come across the claim that we have a moral obligation to "respect" nature, but I'm not sure I know what that means. Is there a difference between "respect-ing" nature and just liking it a whole lot?"*

Marc Lange:

Maybe this will help. Imagine someone who thinks that wild things ought to be preserved and protected—that it is humanity's moral duty to do so. She might even be one of those good people who manages to put these "green" moral principles into action. But suppose that she does not especially enjoy being around natural things. She might well prefer "civilization" to "rough-ing it," and she might not find baby seals especially cute and cuddly. Perhaps she does not even derive any pleas-ure from the thought that there are wild places. They may leave her utterly unmoved, or they may even inspire in her fear and terror. Such an individual might be described as respecting nature without liking it a whole lot.

By the same token, imagine someone who likes nature. She enjoys spending time in wild places and derives deep pleasure from her interactions with wild things. To find opportunities to commune with nature might even be one of her main lifelong pur-suits. She might be as strong an advocate of the national park system as the first person I mentioned, but simply because she would like there to be parks for her to enjoy, not because she feels any moral duty towards nature. Suppose that there is no moral com-ponent at all in her attitude toward nature. She does not think that nature is valuable in any objective or transcendent sense. She may take nature to be valuable to herself, since it is something she likes, but she does not believe that nature is somehow valuable in itself. She simply likes nature, just as I like ice cream. But just as I do not think that someone who is indifferent to ice cream is morally blind, she does not think that someone who is indifferent to nature is morally blind. Such an individual might be described as liking nature but as having no particular respect for nature.

"*Is global warming the most serious threat we face as a planet? If so, what explains the fact that it isn't given top political priority?*"

Thomas Pogge:

Well, I think there are three plausible candidates for the title of most urgent issue on humanity's political agenda. Global warming is one. A substantial change in the global climate, induced by human activities, might well have catastrophic consequences.

The second, somewhat related problem is that of world poverty. Today, the bottom half of humankind are still living in severe poverty, and quite avoidably so: the bottom half of the human income hierarchy have less than 3 percent of global household income and barely 1 percent of global private wealth. Among these people, over 1 billion are reported to be chronically undernourished, 884 million to be without access to safe water, and some 924 million without adequate shelter. Some 18 million of them (including 9 million children under five) die prematurely each year from poverty-related causes, which amounts to nearly one-third of all human deaths. These two problems are related in that—compared to the rest of us, who can prepare and protect ourselves—the global poor are vastly more vulnerable to climate change which already today causes some 300,000 annual deaths among them.

The third problem is that of major wars involving weapons of mass destruction. This problem has receded from public consciousness after the collapse of the Soviet Union, but the overkill capacities of the major powers still exist. And, more disturbingly, many new countries, such as India and Pakistan, have been joining the nuclear club.

I don't think it is especially important to work out which of these three problems is the most urgent. What is important is that all three of them receive far less attention than they merit. Why is this?

One significant factor with regard to problems (1) and (3) is surely the short-term orientation of the world's major agents: corporations, national govern-ments, and their international organizations. Corporate executives are focused on the price of their company's shares in the short term, and politicians are focused on the next elections. Both groups fear that spreading concerns about possible future catastrophes might undermine that on which their success depends: share prices and incumbents' popularity. Problem (2) is a different matter, as this catastrophe is happening right now. It is ignored because it does not hurt the agents that matter: politicians, corporate executives, the mass media, and their paying customers.

To correct the skewed emphasis of our public discourse, ordinary people must take an interest in the important problems and mobilize to place them on the political agenda. Such popular movements exist—a global green movement focusing on climate change, a global anti-poverty movement focusing on the lopsided distribution of the benefits from globalization, and a global peace movement focusing on military aggression, arms exports, and proliferation. These movements are strong enough to make a difference, but they could be much stronger if they had more citizen input and support. We would do better to give such input and support, I think, than to wait for our governments to live up to their most vital responsibilities.

ANIMALS

"*I have a 12-year-old dog. She's no longer in great health, doesn't qualify as cute or attractive, and has rightfully been accused of stinking up any room she remains in for more than a few minutes. Still, she's my dog and I love her. Unfortunately, I am in a situation that requires that I move to a place that won't allow me to bring her. I can't find anyone to take her and am pretty sure that if I take her to the animal shelter she will spend a terrible two weeks there, not be adopted, and then be euthanized. I've been thinking of taking her to a veterinarian who will put her to sleep with a painless injection while I'm there with her. I know this will break my heart, but is it the right thing to do?*"*

Mark Crimmins:

You have what is known in the industry as a Hard Problem. You apparently have already weighed the interests and responsibilities that favor (or as you say, require) your moving without your dog against any prospects of your staying put or moving with her. Presumably you have also exhausted every avenue in searching for a new owner or a rescue operation that might take her.

So let's assume that you really have no alternatives besides immediate euthanasia and a two-week shelter stay probably followed by euthanasia.

To my mind, this is a "weighing" situation, where you need to assess a number of things: the odds (such as they are) that she would find a new home in those two weeks, the value of the life she'd lead if she were to find another owner, the degree of misery she'd likely experience at the shelter, and even the effects on you and on others of knowing that you'd made the decision you did (e.g., would you be haunted by guilt?).

Jay L. Garfield:

I agree that this is a hard one, harder of course for you than it is for us, and harder for you than it is for your dog. The last is an important point. Euthanizing your dog in this situation will cause you a great deal of suffering, but will not cause your dog suffering. It will deprive her of future pleasure of course, but she will not suffer from knowing it (because she won't know it). I think that condemning her to spending her last few weeks without you in a cage, where she will suffer, would be cruel, and so I recommend against that course of action. Of course, if you can, you might arrange a private adoption. But if you can't, I think that euthanasia is the most humane option. You can ease your own feelings of guilt by remembering that. But you probably can't do much about the reasonable grief.

"*Do humans have a greater right to live than other animals? If so, what does that say about how we can and should treat animals? And would beings of much greater intelligence and perception hold that same right over humans?*"

Sally Haslanger:

Good questions! I've been a vegetarian for 38 years and believe that humans should not kill animals for food, clothing or sport. One way to think about this is to ask what it is that makes life valuable. Some think that life itself is valuable, but that isn't plausible given that plants are alive and it doesn't seem to be morally wrong to weed your garden.

Another possibility is that what makes life valuable is sentience. If that's true, then sentient animals (and not plants) would have a moral claim on us, insofar as we have a duty to protect what is valuable. (Though one needs to ask here: what is our duty to protect what is valuable? How far does that duty extend? Are there different sorts of value, some of which have a greater claim on us than others?)

Even if sentience is valuable, however, some argue that humans have capacities that are more valuable still, such as the ability to reason, to value things, to create systems of norms, even morality itself. A challenge arises here, however, since most people would argue that all human beings have equal moral standing, but of course they aren't equal in their abilities to reason, or as you mention, in their intelligence. So what gives humans their special value must be something that humans, qua humans, have, such as being of a kind that has the potential to reason, value, and so forth. Otherwise, we would have a lesser duty to protect infants, the developmentally disabled, the brain injured, etc. The idea is that this potential doesn't come in degrees, but comes with being a member of a certain kind, the human kind, and possibly kinds of more advanced rational, valuing beings we haven't met yet. If what makes life most valuable is this capacity, however, then more advanced beings wouldn't have a greater right to live because they would share this valuable capacity with us.

Even if we allow that humans are more valuable than animals, however, it doesn't follow that humans have a right to kill animals to eat them or wear their skin, or torture them in order to pursue knowledge for its own sake. As long as we grant that sentience is valuable at all, we may have a duty to protect animals from unnecessary pain and suffering. To the extent that we can argue that animals have interests (e.g., not to be killed, not to feel pain, to live a life appropriate to their species), it is plausible that they have a moral claim on us to respect those interests. These are just the first moves in the discussion, however, since many are keen to argue that humans' killing of animals is morally permissible.

As a next step, you might find that Michael Pollan's essay in the *New York Times*, "An Animal's Place," is worth reading.

Richard Heck:

I'll elaborate on the last point. If you are interested in our obligations to animals, and how we ought to treat them, I think it's crucial to recognize that the relevant question here is not: Are the lives of humans more valuable than the lives of other animals? The objection to killing animals need not presuppose that animals' lives and humans' lives are of *equal* value. Most defenders of animal rights would not, I think, hold such a view. Their claim, rather, is that animals' lives are of *sufficiently great* value that they ought not to be killed or, at least, ought not to be killed without a very good reason.

Note that saying that animals *ought not* to be killed does not imply that it is never morally permissible to kill an animal. Humans ought not to be killed, but most people would hold that it is sometimes morally permissible to kill human beings—for example, in self-defense. So if cows' lives are of less value than are the lives of humans, then there may be circumstances in which it is permissible to kill a cow but in which it would not be permissible to kill a human being. But it does not follow from that fact that it is permissible to kill a cow just because you feel like it, or because you would like a leather jacket, or because you would like some filet mignon. Maybe it is permissible to kill a cow for such reasons and maybe it is not, but neither conclusion follows from the fact that cows' lives and humans' lives are not of *equal* value.

"*I'm a vegetarian, but sometimes I find it hard to make the moral case for being veggie. How relevant is it that most of us don't need to eat meat to survive? I find that fact compelling—but of course it doesn't rule out meat-eating across the board. It rules it out just for those of us who don't need to eat meat to survive. Thoughts?*"

Alexander George:

For those of us fortunate to live in industrially advanced Western countries, your claim about being able to have an adequate diet without meat is obviously correct. But that doesn't speak to the moral issue. I'm with you on that one too: I no longer eat meat (I occasionally eat fish, guiltily). If you ask me to offer a defense of this position, I'm not sure I could do it. It's odd: I have a colleague who is quite convinced by some of the arguments for vegetarianism— yet he eats meat. I find all those arguments quite unconvincing—and yet I don't. The relationship between philosophical reflection and daily life can be a complicated thing.

One further thought on this for now. In another post, someone asked about whether torture could be justified in a "ticking bomb" scenario. I believe that these kinds of situations are precisely designed to lead to judgmental paralysis (often because they result in a conflict between several important strands woven into the fabric of some concept). Philosophers are very good at constructing such situations in their attempts to work out what's central to some concept. So that can be a good thing theoretically, but, practically, it can be a disaster because it can encourage us to lose our confidence in our judgments about the vast majority (all?) of real world situations that we face.

So, can we imagine circumstances in which so many important considerations in addition to animal suffering are in play that we're not quite sure what to say about eating animals? Yes, surely. But does that mean that we can't be confident in calling the system of factory farming as it exists right now in the United States a moral outrage? No.

" *Since cheese and yogurt are made from bacteria cultures, which end up dying, is it wrong to eat cheese and yogurt? Or, for that matter, is it wrong to eat plants and anything else that is alive? If so, why do we have laws to protect people, animals, and other complex organisms, but not bacteria, which play just as important a role as do, say, cats?* "

Peter S. Fosl:

What role? Not the role of my companion. And what makes a role important? Note that much of the "role" bacteria plays is that of food for other organisms. Like that of Titus Andronicus, some important roles end in suffering and death.

So, I don't think the concept of "important role" will explain laws prohibiting the killing and tormenting of various organisms. For my own part, I look to three features of organisms that distinguish them from others and justify protections and cultivation: (1) the capacity for conscious suffering; (2) the capacity to engage in projects and practices of value (like writing philosophy, making art, building just societies, sustaining families, advancing learning and wisdom); and (3) the capacity to contribute to the diminishment of conscious suffering and or the support of projects and practices of value. This set of criteria provides a hierarchy of organisms, but not a terribly clean one—and I like that about it. Some bacteria are worthy of protection or cultivation because of (3). Cats share (1) and (3), and maybe a bit of (2). Humans usually (though not always) have (1), (2), and (3) in clear and compelling ways.

Andrew N. Carpenter:

I think Peter is right that the philosophical answer to your question depends on finding a principled way to make judgments about moral considerability: Since our energy and time are finite, we need to decide which things are most worthy of our consideration as we decide what we ought to do.

Suppose that we decided that all living things were equally worthy of moral consideration. Given the sheer number of living things we interact with every day, it would be impossible for us to pay sufficient attention to all of them. In that case, we would either suffer "moral paralysis" or would have to make arbitrary, unprincipled decisions about which beings' moral interests we should care about. This practical problem is worse, of course, if one is inclined to consider non-living things worthy of moral consideration. So, there is a strong practical need to develop and defend criteria for moral considerability.

"What is a good argument for eating meat?"

Peter Smith:

Suppose someone asks: "What is a good argument for drinking wine?" You can survive without wine while still getting the nutrients you require—or at least that's what they tell me. But so what? Wine is a great pleasure to the palate, it makes you feel deliciously intoxicated, and it is a delight to share with family and friends. As Benjamin Franklin said, "Wine is sure proof that God loves us and wants us to be happy." What better reasons could there be for drinking the stuff? If you enjoy wine, that seems to be all the argument you need.

Likewise, let's sit down to, say, a wonderful plate of salami, prosciutto, coppa, and lardo from cinta Senese, followed perhaps by ravioli stuffed with pigeon, then a tagliatta from Val di Chiana beef. Well, food doesn't get much better than that: it is a pleasure to the palate, it makes you feel content and deliciously replete, it is a delight to share with family and friends. What better reasons could there be for eating the stuff?

Maybe you don't like good Tuscan food. Maybe you actually prefer a totally vegetarian diet (Tuscans of course will think you are quite mad). But assuming you do like that sort of carnivorous feast from time to time, on high days and holidays, what further argument do you need for tucking in?

But perhaps you'll say I'm just crassly missing the underlying question. Of course, on the pro side of eating meat of various kinds, there are the wonderful pleasures of the table (just as on the pro side of drinking wine, there are the pleasures of imbibing), and then there's a whole culture bound up with husbandry and hunting. But there is a not inconsiderable con side to meat eating. In particular, there are horrible aspects of factory farming. There are the ecological arguments against using scarce resources to produce some kinds of meat.

Fine. But bringing in those considerations rather changes the issue. The original question seemed to be wondering whether there were any reasons at all to put on the pro-meat-eating side of the scales. Any decent chef can supply such a reason! The revised, and more serious, question is: how do we weigh the evident pro-reasons against the con-reasons? And that question is much disputed. A diet that is low in meat overall, with the meat decently sourced (and coming largely from animals like sheep or wild boar raised on marginal land) is what the balance of reasons inclines me to. Others of course differ in their conclusions.

RELIGION

"*Should all morality based on authority, such as the command of God, be rejected? Acting morally because one fears punishment or anticipates rewards in the afterlife is repugnant, because one is motivated purely by self-interest. And acting morally because some person or some religious text tells one to is also repugnant, because one is motivated by blind conformity.*"

Matthew Silverstein:

It seems clear that the force of morality cannot depend on the coercive sort of authority you describe, whether that authority is wielded by God or by the state. God's threats of punishment carry no more moral weight than anybody else's. And so if murder is wrong because God forbids it, God's authority must extend beyond his (admittedly impressive) power to cast us into hell for all eternity.

The sort of authority that morality is supposed to have is not the coercive authority of reward and punishment, but rather what philosophers often call *normative authority*. (Precisely what this sort of authority amounts to remains the subject of much philosophical disagreement.) Many philosophers think that normative authority must ultimately be independent of God's will and commands. Thus it seems that any compelling account of the foundations of morality is going to have a humanistic rather than a religious basis. One of the great challenges of moral philosophy is to explain how such foundations are possible. How can any commandment or law—of divine or human origin—have genuine normative authority?

" *If I am an atheist, should I try (while remaining civil) to convince religious people that they are wrong?* "

Alexander George:

It all depends on how persistent, intrusive, and manipulative the trying is. In so far as the convincing is none of these, it sounds like it would give rise to just the kind of fascinating conversations that contribute to life's interest.

Peter Smith:

"To every thing there is a season, and a time to every purpose under the heaven" (Ecclesiastes 3:1). There are occasions when it might be appropriate to talk and argue about atheism, or about vegetarianism, or global warming, or liberalism, or the Welsh rugby team, or whatever else grips you, and other occasions when it certainly wouldn't be. Just going around trying to convince people of your views, willy-nilly, is not to treat others with much respect, nor is it likely to be very productive.

But I take it that isn't what's being suggested! The issue, I imagine, is: if you have come to believe that some widely shared, deeply held view is wrong, then should you press your contrary arguments on appropriate occasions, even if people are prone to get a bit upset/offended? Should you, for example, when the occasion is suitable, advance your atheistic arguments even if it rocks the boat?

Well, why not? It is only through reasoning things through, back and forth, propounding arguments, and listening to counter-arguments, that knowledge advances. And I'm still old-fashioned enough to think that we need all the knowledge we can get.

Gabriel Segal:

Quite so. I think it depends in part on who the religious people are. If there is almost no chance that you will change their views then there is no reason why you should spend your time and energy on the matter. And

I expect this applies to a lot of people. If there is a decent chance that you will change their views, then a good question is: would it benefit them? I expect that the answer will often be "yes." If I had once been religious and someone had convinced me that I was wrong, I'd be grateful. Lots of us want to know the truth.

"I live in a Muslim country, and around here there are lots of disagreements between religious and non-religious people about the limits of freedom. Religious people often claim to be offended by certain behavior—for example, some religious people say that they feel offended when someone nearby drinks an alcoholic drink. On the other hand, the non-religious people say that it is their freedom to drink alcoholic drinks. How should we think about these issues? Are there general principles about limits of freedom that we can use to solve such cases?"

Peter S. Fosl:

This is a terribly important issue. Luckily, there has been quite a lot of work done on the topic. Two general principles to consider are these: (1) With regard to personal conduct like food, drink, sex, ornament, dress, etc., one should be at liberty to do whatever one pleases so long as no one else is harmed by the conduct; and (2) liberty should be maximized.

One of the sticky bits here is the notion of *harm*. Isn't being offended a kind of harm? Yes, I think it can be, but things get complicated here. In some cases, the concept of *offense* is misused. It may be in the case you describe. Can one be offended by conduct that is not directed at one or a group to which one belongs? One can be upset, one can be disgusted, one can be outraged, but I'm not sure that offense is the right concept to use in the case you describe. It's also unclear why even if one can be said to be offended by conduct not directed at oneself or a group to which one belongs that drinking alcoholic beverages should be regarded as counting as offensive. Aside from the fact that many Muslims around the world find the practice to be consistent with Islam, shouldn't the faithful, instead of offense, feel pity or sadness for those who consume alcoholic beverages? Should Christians be offended that Muslims use the Qu'ran in worship, or don't take communion? No. There's nothing offensive, so far as I can see, in someone's not practicing one's religion or in practicing no religion at all.

Is there harm of another sort? For example, does the practice of other religions or the refusal to practice any religion harm the adherents of one's religion by making it easier for that religion to fade and go extinct? Does an atheist's drinking alcohol in public encourage non-drinking Muslims to abandon or weaken their faith? Do blasphemy and anti-religious discourse pose threats to the faith? Perhaps. But I don't think these actions can be regarded as harms to an individual believer. It's not a harm to change someone's mind about an issue, and it's not a harm for one religion to go out of favor or for all religions to come to be regarded as nonsense. In the contest of ideas and practices in a free society, some will prevail and persist, while others will go extinct and cease to exist. If the religious wish their beliefs and practices to persist, they should try to persuade others to adhere to them. They should not, however, use force or coercion to prevent those who disagree from acting otherwise. And they should accept the possibility that even present adherents to the religion will change their minds, join other religions, or abandon religion altogether. Accepting these possibilities is a precondition for life in a free society. And accepting these possibilities makes for a much happier society, too.

"*Is teaching religion in public schools morally wrong?*"

David Brink:

It probably depends on what you have in mind as "teaching religion." You might have in mind teaching comparative religions or the study of a particular religion as a cultural and/or historical phenomenon. If so, then I don't see why teaching religion, in this sense, is wrong, at least if it is offered as an elective rather than a requirement. However, you might have in mind teaching religion in a way that represents theistic claims as true and/or advocates some religious doctrines rather than others. It seems to me that this is probably wrong in multiple ways.

First, it is *legally* wrong in the United States because it violates the anti-establishment clause of the First Amendment, requiring a separation of church and state. But there seem to be good moral reasons for this constitutional guarantee, so it seems likely to be *morally* wrong as well. Whether to believe religious claims at all and, if so, which ones seem to be matters of conscience and are subject to persistent, intractable debate that is resistant to resolution. In such circumstances, there seem to be strong moral reasons to tolerate differences of religious belief, in part by relegating their influence to a sphere of private conduct and concern. Moreover, there is a powerful moral tradition that thinks that we need to condition the exercise of the coercive power of the state on the ability to justify burdens that it imposes on some citizens in terms that it would be reasonable for them to understand and accept. It is arguable that this constraint of public justification rules out state action that rests on religious belief, inasmuch as religious belief seems to rely on faith, rather than evidence or secular justification.

THE POLITICAL

JUSTICE

"*Some people are born into privilege, and some people into poverty. Do you think that those unfortunate enough to be in the second group are sometimes justified in resorting to crime, such as civil disobedience or theft, either through frustration or necessity? And if they do resort to crime, is it fair to judge and punish them in the same way that more privileged people who do the same thing are judged?*"

Thomas Pogge:

Extreme contrasts of privilege and poverty are often the result of unjust social institutions, such as feudalism and serfdom. In such a context, people in dire poverty may well be justified in violating their society's property laws, in practicing civil disobedience, and even in overthrowing the established order, because those laws and this order lack moral standing. But even in a context of severe social injustice, it is not morally permissible to violate any and all laws (e.g., by killing children or by stealing from people even poorer than oneself).

Those administering and enforcing the laws in a seriously unjust society will rarely admit that these laws are seriously unjust and that some violations of them are justified. Still, they ought to reflect on the justice of the laws they apply and enforce, and if they find the justice of some of these laws to be dubious, they should conclude that they ought to punish leniently if at all. They ought also to reflect on the state of mind of the defendant, and if they find her to be motivated by a conscientious and well-founded conviction that she permissibly violated unjust laws, they should (even if they disagree) decide on a more lenient punishment or even on acquittal. In some cases, the conscientious and not unreasonable conviction that a law is unjust, even if incorrect, may be considered an excuse in mitigation of blame and punishment.

Even in a just social context, people may experience severe frustration or great need. In such a context, violating the law is generally not justifiable, but it may nonetheless be excusable in certain cases. It may be excusable, for example, for a poor mother to steal a sweet or a small toy because she can ill afford to buy a holiday gift for her child. (This may be excusable to some extent even if it was her own responsibility that she ran out of money before month's end.) In such a case it would be fair to blame and punish her less, if at all, even while a similar theft by a more affluent person

117

is blamed and punished more severely. Here, once again, the relevant difference lies in the defendant's state of mind. Such excuses are recognized in many civilized legal systems.

> " Many communities in the world are populated by the descendents of aggressive invaders, but we do not hold these people responsible for the atrocities their ancestors committed. For example, most reasonable people would not blame modern Americans for the mass murder of the Native Americans. On what grounds, then, could the descendents of the aggressive invaders be said to owe anything to the descendents of the invaded? "

Jay L. Garfield:

It is useful to distinguish between blame and responsibility. One may not be to blame for a set of actions taken by one's ancestors, but if one benefits from them, and another is harmed by them, one might still morally owe reparations.

For example, suppose that my parents stole all of your parents' wealth, and left it to me. I'm now quite rich, and you're destitute. I'm not to blame for what my parents did—I didn't steal anything—and likewise you're not the victim of any theft. But there is still a strong case to be made that I am in possession of stolen goods that rightly belong to you, and that I owe you reparations.

Now, the more distant the harms are from current circumstances, the harder it gets to assign particular benefits and injuries. But the more immediate cases, or those where, despite the passage of time, the benefits and burdens remain clearly traceable, might well demand reparation, even if they don't demand guilt.

"*I am a Zimbabwean student studying in South Africa, and like many I am deeply distressed by the events of Zimbabwe's recent past. I am particularly opposed to the blinding lights of patriotism and nationalism because of their repressive and destructive effects. But I also feel that much of my distress and my desire for change in Zimbabwe is motivated by the very patriotism I tend to abhor. Is nationalism ever justified?*"

Allen Stairs:

All of us take ourselves to have special obligations toward people with whom we have special relationships. Other things being equal, I take my obligations to my friends, my family and my colleagues to be stronger and more extensive than my obligations to strangers. Indeed, these sorts of relationships are an important part of what makes life meaningful for most of us. But that sort of meaning gets spread beyond the circle of people we actually know. Most of us feel a special connection with communities whose members are mostly unknown to us—colleagues in other departments, citizens of our home towns, members of associations we belong to, and so on. Obviously this can extend to nations as well.

My first suggestion, then, is that you shouldn't feel guilty about the fact that some of your distress about the situation in Zimbabwe is based on something like patriotism. You do have a special relationship with Zimbabwe, after all. That said, your hesitation is no doubt based on the fact that patriotism and nationalism have been the source of a good deal of the world's misery. That's a fact that we can't be reminded of too often. Our fellow-feeling for our compatriots should never be allowed to turn itself into hostility toward those outside our circle, or to aggression.

So I would say that "justified" may not be the most useful word. It's permissible to have a special sympathy for one's compatriots, but not permissible to let that be the basis for aggression toward other people, nor for taking one's own nation to have special rights and privileges in the world.

One last note: on reflection, we might even think that our capacity for patriotic sentiment can lead us to expand rather than contract our sympathies. If I can care about countrymen whom I will never meet, then I am no doubt capable of expanding that circle of care well beyond national boundaries.

Thomas Pogge:
It's worth distinguishing two very different kinds of nationalism or, more broadly, partiality. The first is

well-expressed by the saying "my country, right or wrong." Here the agent is a nationalist or patriot by putting the interests (crudely conceived) of a certain group above those of others and above morality. With the second kind of nationalism or partiality, the agent puts an especially high value on the moral quality of a certain group or of certain special others.

To illustrate, consider how a parent may respond to the discovery that her son has stolen toys from a little store in the neighborhood. Family partiality of the first kind may lead the parent to help ensure that the theft is not discovered (even while this parent would not give similar help to stealing children of another household). Family partiality of the second kind may lead the parent to ask the son to bring the toys back and to apologize to the shopkeeper (even while this parent would make no effort to impart such a character lesson to stealing children of another household).

In your Zimbabwe case, both kinds of nationalism may be in play. As a citizen of the country, you may have special affection for your compatriots. This first kind of nationalism may lead you to hope for an end of the dictatorship and of the enormous suffering it inflicts on your compatriots. The second kind of nationalism may lead you to work toward a more just Zimbabwe, one with decent political leaders, just social institutions, and morally alert citizens. In the case at hand, these two ends fit well together. But the two kinds of nationalism may come apart on some other occasions, as when you must decide whether to support an unjust attack by your country upon a weaker neighbor whose resources Zimbabwe might appropriate. Here the first kind of nationalist would support the attack; the second would oppose it.

You can endorse patriotism of the second kind, and accept a special responsibility to promote a more just Zimbabwe, without endorsing the first kind of patriotism that you (rightly, in my view) tend to abhor.

"*Egalitarian principles suggest that it is important to provide equal opportunities for all. But the more I think about it, the more I think this leads to really strange consequences. Does this mean that, for instance, every continent should get an equal number of soccer teams into the World Cup, despite the fact that some continents clearly display a higher standard of soccer?*"

Jyl Gentzler:

When we're attracted to a principle of equality of opportunity, we're often moved by the thought that everyone should have the same chance to gain access to the good things in life. Of course, if people blow their chances, then they have no one to blame but themselves. But they might reasonably complain if their access to the good things of life is due to factors over which they have no control.

But what, then, about my access to the NBA? I'm 5' 2", and while not entirely graceless, I'm not exactly the picture of athleticism. Is it unfair that the NBA excludes me from its ranks? It's surely not my fault that I have the height that I have. So has the NBA violated some right that I have to equal opportunity?

The reasoning here, of course, goes much too quickly. It seems entirely appropriate that access to jobs is determined by one's ability to do the job well (even if one's ability to do a particular job is due to factors outside of one's own control). We wouldn't want surgeons or even basketball players to be incompetent, since our lives or the quality of our lives depends on the competence of others. Since we all benefit from having competent people in positions on which the quality of our own life depends, it is reasonable for us all to agree to have access to these positions depend on skill. And so we tend to understand our right to an equality of opportunity to certain jobs as compatible with discrimination on the basis of skill, though not on the basis of attributes like skin color that have nothing to do with skill.

But what about access to the good things in life? In our society, access to certain jobs and access to the good things of life are not unrelated. Certain jobs just *are* more rewarding financially, intellectually, emotionally, and socially than others. There's nothing to be done about the intrinsic rewards of different jobs, but what about the extrinsic rewards—what, for example, about compensation? Is it fair that different levels of compensation are associated with different jobs? Is it fair that access to essentials like healthcare is linked to access to different jobs? Here's where you get real disagreement among philosophers about the implications of our commitment to a principle of equality of opportunity.

RIGHTS

"*If someone feels no remorse over his hurtful actions, is incapable of feeling love, and has no interest in other people apart from using them for selfish means, does this person have humanity? And if this person doesn't—and human rights is a concept of "shared humanity," as Ronald Dworkin says—does he have the same human rights as other human beings?*"

Thomas Pogge:

Human beings can and do change. They may lack important attributes at one time and yet come to possess them later. So we must choose whether to tie the ascription of humanity in the relevant sense to attributes they have or to ones they are capable of having.

I think we should choose the latter option. Only if we do can we firmly include infants and small children within the domain of humanity and human rights. Moreover, we should guard against our susceptibility to error, especially when we feel anger and hostility. We should avoid demonizing those we hold in contempt, and we should honor our own humanity by treating them humanely rather than as beasts that may be subjected to any imaginable form of torture and degradation. (The possibilities of error and demonization are amply and shockingly exemplified in the horrors committed in Abu Ghraib.) If their full humanity can emerge at all, this is most likely to happen through treating them humanely, not through definitively giving up on them.

What then must we believe a being to be capable of to merit human rights and humane treatment? I do not think we should require a capacity for emotions such as love and remorse. A capacity for moral judgment and conduct should suffice. So long as someone can restrain, or can yet come to restrain, her conduct by reference to moral considerations, we should regard her as meriting human rights.

I propose this as a sufficient condition, not a necessary one. I do not think we should deny human rights to human beings who fail the test proposed. Those who permanently lack the capacity for moral judgment and conduct—the severely mentally disabled—should also be treated humanely and be afforded human rights (though some human rights, such as those to political participation, freedom of expression, etc., may lack application in their case).

"One thing that I have often heard is that "You can't have rights without responsibilities," and I wondered if you could explain the reasoning behind that statement. Is it something that can be deduced using philosophy, or is it merely an assertion?"

Thomas Pogge:

Rights give each of us claims on the conduct of others. Your right not to be tortured requires others to respect this right: not to torture you, not to order or abet your torture, and to organize their society so that you are safe from torture. Denying that others have such responsibilities is tantamount to denying that you have the right.

This reasoning may not quite get us to the statement you query. It shows only that, for you to have rights, *others* must have responsibilities. But then it would be immorally self-centered for you to insist that you have rights that entail responsibilities for others and that no one else has rights that entail responsibilities for you. The last step is then a moral step. It is *possible* for someone to have rights but no responsibilities. But such a situation would be morally unacceptable because it would give this person a special moral status that could not be shared by others. For if everyone had no responsibilities, then no one would have rights.

GOVERNMENT

"I've been wondering a long time about this and I can't come up with an answer. Hopefully you can help me. What is the point of government?"

Alexander George:

The short answer that many political philosophers (such as Thomas Hobbes, John Locke, and John Rawls) have offered is that we are all far better off in a civil society structured by basic institutions (legal, economic, political) that constitute the government than we would be if we were left on our own. Hobbes and Locke called the condition in which man does not live under a government the State of Nature. Both believed that living in the State of Nature was far more uncomfortable and dangerous than living under a government. In fact, Hobbes famously wrote (in his *Leviathan*) that life in the State of Nature would be "solitary, poor, nasty, brutish and short."

"Is there really a social contract? To begin with, how can we consent to be governed by a government that has

a monopoly over a region? And if there is a social contract, is the government upholding its end of the bargain? Presumably, we would agree to the contract in order to gain protection, among other things. But many Supreme Court cases have upheld that the government is not liable to protect you in lots of situations. "

Lorraine Besser-Jones:

In thinking about the existence of a social contract, or lack thereof, the first thing we need to do is separate questions about the possible terms of the contract from questions about the existence of the contract. You note that courts have denied that the members of the government can always be held liable to protect individuals; these rulings on their own, however, don't give us reason to believe either for or against the existence of a social contract. For example, rather than suggesting the lack of a social contract, the rulings could reflect the terms of the contract, and in particular, that absolute protection is not one of the terms. And this would be reasonable: we typically think that the terms of the contract should be limited, at the very least, by what is within each party's capacities. It is not always within the government's capacity to be both fully informed of possible threats and prepared to protect individuals from those threats.

Your overall concern about the very existence of a social contract is a pressing one. There is a real sense in which the government does have a monopoly over us. We cannot opt out of the government's jurisdiction—even if we choose to move from one country to another, we are subject to the new government's policies. Traditionally, philosophers who are sympathetic to the idea of the social contract have tried to show that the contract exists in virtue of some sort of non-explicit form of consent that we give. So, for example, John Locke has argued in favor of the notion of tacit consent, whereby we (tacitly) consent to the rules of a particular government in light of residing in its territory or otherwise making use of its resources. Others have argued in favor of a hypothetical social contract, whereby consent is deemed to exist if we can establish, on hypothetical grounds, that agents would have consented to it.

Most philosophers believe that if a social contract does exist in contemporary society, it does so as a result of some non-explicit form of consent. However, many philosophers are skeptical about the viability and legitimacy of these forms of consent, and this skepticism leads them to argue that there is no social contract. They are thus left with the task of showing either that the government can be justified via other means, or that the government cannot be justified.

" *Do I have a moral responsibility to submit accurate tax returns? If my government is managing society for the benefit of a small elite or using tax money to invade smaller countries with lies as a pretext, surely at least some portion of my taxes does not rightly belong to it."*

Thomas Pogge:

Most citizens, nearly all, disagree with some government expenditures. They think it's wrong to tax us for agricultural or opera subsidies, for drug rehabilitation, for foreign aid, for nuclear weapons, or a few thousand other things. Now we could all cheat on our taxes, retaining from what we legally owe the proportion that corresponds to the expenditures of which we disapprove (or disapprove on moral grounds). Or we could defer to governmental expenditure decisions reached through our democratic political process.

Once the issue is presented in this more general way, it is clear that there is moral reason to comply with majority decisions one disapproves of—even those that one *morally* disapproves of. In a democracy, if you find laws or policies morally objectionable, you ought to present your arguments to your fellow citizens and persuade them to change such laws and policies with you. To be sure, such efforts often fail. But the whole point of democracy is that we defer to majority decisions. Without such deference, there would be little point in voting in the first place.

This presumption in favor of deference becomes weaker the less democratic the relevant political system is. If it is formally democratic but so dominated by money that many citizens stand no chance of influencing decisions about policies or office holders, then the presumption of deference is weaker, at least in the case of these politically marginalized people. If some people are disenfranchised, then the presumption may fail completely in their case. If the political system is dictatorial, then I see really no moral reason for deference on the part of the subjects.

Even when the presumption in favor of deference is at full strength, it can be overcome. Using tax money to invade a smaller country with lies as a pretext and a few hundred thousand dead civilians is a case in point. A very good case can be made that, when Hitler attacked Poland in this fashion in 1939, German citizens were no longer morally required to pay the full taxes they legally owed. In fact, a good case can be made that they were no longer morally *permitted* to pay *any* taxes or give any other form of support, such as enlisting in the armed forces. (Consider that, if you withhold 4 percent of your taxes on the ground that this is the percentage of Federal expenditure destined for Iraq, this revenue loss will in fact be spread over the entire government operation. You will have reduced your contribution to the Iraq war by a mere 4 percent.)

We can lastly consider the question *how* one may or should withhold one's taxes. One can do this sneakily, by submitting an inaccurate return. One can do it openly as an act of civil disobedience: by filing an accurate return and then refusing to pay some or all of what one legally owes. Or one can do it openly and legally by reducing the taxes one legally owes—for instance, by taking early retirement or by making tax-deductible charitable donations or by moving abroad. Such open (legal or illegal) tax reductions have the advantage that they are not easily mistaken for selfish choices, and they also afford an opportunity to appeal to the moral conscience of one's fellow citizens. If 1 percent of a country's citizens stopped paying their taxes in open opposition to a grave injustice, they might well make this injustice much harder to sustain. And likewise if 1 percent left the country in open protest of its policies. By contrast, if 1 percent secretly cheat on their taxes, they just raise the level of tax evasion a bit with little political effect.

"*Is scientific research a good use of government funding when hospitals, schools and social services are suffering from tight budgets?*"

Jasper Reid:

There is a certain irony in seeing such a question posted online, typed in via a computer (or, for all I know, maybe some even more cutting-edge piece of handheld technology). Because, if wise men and women, the best part of a century ago, hadn't developed the principles of quantum mechanics, there could be no such things. At least not in anything like their current form: we'd still be on valves and transistors, or even cogs and pulleys, themselves the off-shoots of yet earlier scientific research. As for those hospitals you mention, had it not been for scientific research into human biology, they wouldn't have any treatments to offer their patients (in which case, it really wouldn't matter if their budgets were to be taken away altogether!). Gene therapy, for instance, clearly would not have been able to get off the ground if its developers had not possessed any conception of a gene or understood the structure of DNA. But we owe all of this knowledge to state-funded scientific research.

Scientific discoveries do much more than merely satisfy our intellectual curiosity. The chief value of scientific research lies in the fact that it facilitates technological research, and technological research can lead in turn to colossal benefits for every single part of society. Now, some scientific research is deliberately tied to very specific technological applications— and, consequently, such research is often funded by commercial interests. But even "pure" scientific research does often lead, in a more indirect way, to major technological advances. The purer the science, the harder it is to predict what *specific* technological applications it might eventually issue, and so it is perfectly understandable that the corporations might be reluctant to fund it themselves. So it is lucky for us that someone—government—is willing to do so. Because, when I say that the results can benefit every single part of society, I really do mean *every* part. While comfortable folks in the developed world get to enjoy their computers, the developing world still faces the perennial problems of famine, malaria, etc.; and climate change is a major worry for all of us. Now, the question of whether or not there is a genuine *will* to solve such problems is a political matter, unfortunately resting on human foibles. But, as to whether there might be a *way* to solve them (and, if so, then what way that might be), for that I'd be inclined to look to the scientists.

"*Recently, a politician running for re-election announced that he supports a major government initiative that would bring money and jobs to my area. If the initiative passed, my life would almost certainly improve. The rest of the country, however, would be worse off, because the plan is mostly pork spending that focuses a disproportionate amount of money on one small area. At first I thought I should vote for the candidate who opposes the initiative, because that would help the most people. But on the other hand, our political system seems to expect citizens to vote according to their regional interests, and is designed to balance these competing interests. Our congress, for instance, is elected on a state-by-state basis, implying that each congressperson should have a special concern for their state. What is the responsible way to vote?"*

Thomas Pogge:

I don't think geographical representation implies what you say it does. Its rationale could just as easily be that the legislature—when deliberating about justice and the common good for all Americans—should be fully informed of how its decisions would affect people in different parts of the country. Each legislator would then bring her or his special knowledge and understanding into the debate, but they all would decide on a common basis of what's best for all citizens.

This would be, in my view, a much better system than the one we have, where legislators are beholden to the interests of their specific electorates and contributors (often actually more to the campaign contributors from outside their district than to ordinary people within their district). But it does not follow that you must therefore act in the interest of all citizens, impartially. You can say that, even if it were best if everyone were impartial, citizens and their political representatives are not in fact impartial and, because most of them pay no heed to your interests, it's permissible for you to pay no heed to their interests.

But do you want to make this plea? Your first reaction shows that you find the more impartial stance morally more appealing. So you should perhaps do your bit to get us there—for example, by not punishing candidates who take an impartial perspective, by not rewarding those who bring wasteful pork to your district, and by discussing different ideas of democracy with those around you.

LAW

"*Why should society put such a high value on the act of taking an oath? We take an oath to say the truth, to become a citizen, to take public office, to serve on a commission, etc. But an oath is only as good as a person taking the oath—after all, it is not difficult to say an oath insincerely, as a matter of convenience, and then turn around and violate it. So what's the difference between doing something under oath and doing it not under oath? Should we expect a higher level of integrity for actions done under oath because of the ceremonious nature of oath-taking?*"

Richard Heck:

One way to think about oaths would be to regard them as a ritualized form of *promising*. If so, then one aspect of these questions is: What's the significance of promises? There's a difference between saying that one plans to do something and *promising* to do it. Simply saying that one plans to do something can certainly create reasonable expectations that one will do it, and that can in turn create moral obligations to do it. But promising to do a thing creates a moral obligation to do it that does not in any way depend upon other people's expecting that one will do it. One purpose of oaths, then, might just be to create the sorts of moral duties a promise would. (Of course, whether one who makes a promise, or takes an oath, takes those duties seriously is another matter.)

Another aspect of the questions is: Why should promise-making be ritualized as an oath? I can think of two kinds of answers worth exploring. One might be that the public and ritual character of oath-taking encourages people to take it seriously. Another might be that the ritual form creates *legal* obligations as well as moral ones. It's one thing to lie and quite another to lie on the stand, and part of the point of the witness's oath might be (i) to create the difference and (ii) to make that difference vivid.

   I recently read an article in which a lawyer referred to something called "role morality" in defending his behavior, which was not especially good. What is "role morality," and what school or body of philosophy does it belong to? It seemed somewhat bogus when presented as an excuse for behavior that would otherwise be called immoral. Is there really a different moral system for lawyers?"

Thomas Pogge:

We sometimes play certain social roles in which it is morally appropriate to disregard certain otherwise weighty considerations and to give great weight to others that one could otherwise disregard.

Examples? A trustee should try to find the best possible investments for her ward without regard to how such investments would affect the value of her own portfolio. A judge or juror should set aside her likes and dislikes of certain kinds of people. A legislator should disregard the impact that pending legislation would have on her son's business. The common idea here is that important social purposes are best promoted if the occupants of certain roles understand them in these ways.

The lawyer's role is somewhat unusual because it is part of an adversarial system. The idea behind such a system is that the socially best outcome is achieved when some of the protagonists do not aim for it, but for something quite different. To get the most exciting soccer match, we need players focused *not* on making the match as exciting as possible, but players focused on winning. To get just and fair outcomes in the courtroom, we need lawyers focused *not* on getting just and fair outcomes, but on winning their case. That's the theory.

It is immediately clear that, in an adversarial system, the role players' conduct must be constrained. Players and lawyers should try to win, but not by bribing the referee or judge, and not by poisoning their opponents. Still, within these constraints, players and lawyers may fight pretty hard and one-sidedly for their own side.

The lawyers' role morality raises interesting ethical issues when a lawyer's behavior hurts not the opposing side (which, ideally at least, has its own lawyer), but innocent third parties. Thus, a lawyer's best way to get her client off the hook may be to "destroy" an elderly witness or to suggest without a shred of evidence that a rape victim is a "loose woman." Lawyers like to think that their role morality permits or even mandates such conduct on their part. But I do not think it is plausible to hold that a lawyer may or should do on her client's behalf what it would be wrong for this client to do on his own behalf. If it would be wrong for a rapist to try to get a more lenient sentence by making wholly ungrounded suggestions about the "looseness" of his victim's "sexual morals," then it would be wrong for his lawyer to make such wholly ungrounded suggestions for the same purpose.

"Is it ever legitimate to prohibit an action by law solely because it offends part of the population?"

Thomas Pogge:

John Stuart Mill argued that offense to others is not a permissible ground for a legal prohibition of conduct: "The only purpose for which power can be rightfully exercised over any member of a civilized community, against his will, is to prevent harm to others. His own good, either physical or moral, is not a sufficient reason." (*On Liberty*, Chapter 1) But Mill also stretched the notion of harm in various ways so as to reaffirm prevailing prejudices about what conduct it is permissible to proscribe. To think about your question carefully, one needs to start with a sharp definition of *offense* that supports a clear distinction between *offense* and *harm*. This is a difficult task, and it is quite likely that our linguistic intuitions about what is harm and what is mere offense are shaped by our moral intuitions about what may and may not rightfully be proscribed by the criminal law.

Most people in developed Western countries find deeply offensive and want to see criminalized conduct of the following kinds, even when all parties immediately involved have freely given their consent: polygamy, pederasty, incest, necrophilia, the eating of dead human beings, human sacrifices, and physician-assisted suicide. In which of these cases can the majority adduce a justification for prohibition other than offense? In which of these cases, in particular, can the majority plausibly claim to be harmed by the offensive conduct or claim that willing participants in this conduct are being harmed unduly (in a way not justifiable by their consent)? Such claims have been made about every one of the listed cases, and the assessment of these claims then depends on one's definition of harm as distinct from mere offense.

"*How far does the right to privacy extend? Recently, at one of the most popular public beaches in Australia, a man was arrested and fined $500 for surreptitiously photographing women who were lying on the sand with no tops on. Many people using this beach freely choose to sunbathe topless, and the man admitted that he wanted the photos just for personal gratification. Although I think the man's behavior was in poor taste, I can't see why it should be held illegal or punishable. If it is permissible for passers-by to see a person on Bondi Beach who has chosen to disrobe, then why should it be impermissible for passers-by to take photographs? If the sunbathers do not wish people to photograph their bodies, shouldn't they just keep themselves covered while they are in public?*"

Nicholas D. Smith:

As a matter of prudence, I am inclined to agree with your arguments—if one does not want others to photograph one's exposed breasts (or other body parts), one should keep them covered in public.

On the other hand, I don't think that the issue is quite as simple as this. The man who was arrested admitted that he used the photos for his own sexual gratification. But what if he was posting them on a website, or selling them for profit? I think there are somewhat thorny issues here, and that the most important ones have to do with legal protections of personal privacy, and where the lines get drawn on this issue. Does appearing in public mean that anyone can photograph me for any purpose whatsoever? That does seem a bit too much! Here is another example: what do you think of a pedophile who photographs children running around on a beach in the nude, as one can see in lots of places in the world? No problem here? I guess I would caution the questioner that the obviously prudent reply that he or she provides masks some important issues about whether our privacy should still be protected from various forms of intrusion even when we are in public. And I guess my own intuitions on this are somewhat mixed. Although I agree they should not be as aggressively protected as when we are in private, I don't think it becomes "open season" when we are in public, either, no matter what we are or are not wearing.

" *We recently learned about racial profiling in my social studies class. While I agree that it is unethical to assume that all people of a certain race are criminals, there did seem to be some logic behind the idea that*

I didn't want to bring up in class. I am not a racist and am in fact involved in closing the achievement gap in my school district, and I'm hoping I can ask my question here without being judged.

If statistics show that for whatever unfair reason (maybe because of discrimination), a greater percentage of people of race A become alcoholics or grow up in poverty or something, and statistics also show that alcoholics or people who grow up in poverty are more likely to commit crimes, then isn't it only logical to conclude that a randomly-chosen person of race A is more likely to be a criminal than a randomly-chosen person of race B?"

Thomas Pogge:

First of all, I think it's good you bring this up. Better to discuss such matters openly than to pretend they don't exist.

One should be clearer, perhaps, about the step from belief to action. Surely many things correlate with race, gender, or religion; and we may notice these correlations and form beliefs about them and perhaps even test these beliefs through large-scale data collection. In some cases, the mere researching of such correlations is morally dubious, by fostering contempt for a group even while serving no legitimate social purpose.

But in the case of crimes, there is a legitimate social purpose: crime avoidance through deterrence and apprehension. So it is hard to deny that knowing more about the people who tend to commit certain kinds of crimes can be useful. But then how useful such knowledge will be depends on what one would be able and morally permitted to do with it if one had it.

In the case of serious crimes there is, I think, a clear presumption in favor of using such knowledge and hence of acquiring it. If those who commit a certain kind of serious crime in some city are described (by the victims and witnesses) as predominantly fitting a certain profile, then it makes sense to concentrate scarce police resources on people fitting this profile. To take an extreme example, if virtually all rapes and attempted rapes in some city are reportedly committed by males, then it makes little sense to have half of the plainclothes anti-rape task force trailing females.

Criminal profiling of African Americans is different in three important respects. First, insofar as correlations exist, they tend to be much weaker than just described. Second, there is a long-standing history of severe discrimination and disadvantage the ongoing social and psychological effects of which racial profiling is likely to aggravate. Third, those engaging in (perhaps expressly authorized) racial profiling may have a certain degree of racism that may influence their racial profiling in ways that unduly harm African Americans and in turn deepen the profilers' racism.

These three considerations may typically be weighty enough to disqualify most actual racial profiling that has taken place. But I don't think they can show that racial profiling is wrong in principle or even merely always wrong in this country. There may be cases where racial profiling is likely to be highly effective in reducing serious crime even while its costs are much lower than usual. For example, consider a city that is racially mixed and where blacks are highly overrepresented among those who commit and also among those who fall victim to a certain crime. Suppose a special task force is formed to combat this type of crime, and suppose it is an all-black force. In this case, the three considerations against racial profiling are much weaker than usual, and it is certainly arguable that racial profiling can proceed so long as it really does prove highly effective against the serious crime in question.

PUNISHMENT

"Do you think a crime committed against a schoolteacher should carry a greater punishment than the same crime committed against a drug dealer? In other words, should a victim's character be taken into account when sentencing?"

Oliver Leaman:

No, character should play no part in sentencing. Nor indeed should social standing or moral standing. We might think that the schoolteacher in question was more deserving of our sympathy than the drug dealer, but sentencing should be based on what the criminal deserves to receive, not on the qualities of the victim.

On a consequentialist view of punishment we might seek to protect some social groups by punishing crimes against them disproportionately, and then we would need an argument as to why the effects of such a policy would be particularly desirable. But many would feel that such a policy reveals what is wrong with consequentialism in ethics, since it deviates from aligning punishment with desert.

"Should the punishment for attempted murder be as severe as the punishment for murder? If your ethical scheme is based on universal moral principles, surely whatever is bad about trying to kill someone is bad regardless of whether the would-be murderer happens to succeed. And if you are a consequentialist, it seems that we should protect the populace by imprisoning those who try to kill people, regardless of whether they happen to succeed."

Thomas Pogge:

Here are two different arguments a consequentialist might make.

(1) Suppose all attempted murders are punished equally, regardless of success, with each attempt being punished with 6 years in jail and 30 percent of punished attempts being successful. Now consider this reform: We increase punishment for successful attempts from 6 to 13 years and decrease punishments for unsuccessful attempts from 6 to 3 years. This reform leaves constant the jail time per punished attempt (which consequentialists typically count as a negative): $13 \times 30\% + 3 \times 70\% = 6$. (Obviously, the numbers here are just for illustration.) But the reform is likely to increase deterrence, because prospective murderers are going to focus more on the "successful" outcome that risks a 13-year penalty than on the "unsuccessful" outcome that risks a 3-year penalty, even though the latter outcome is more likely. As a result of better deterrence, fewer murder attempts are made, fewer people are murdered, and fewer years are spent in jail. (Obviously, for this argument to work, I must be right about the psychology of prospective murderers.)

(2) Whether an attempted murder succeeds or not is sometimes due to luck. But it is often correlated with features of the agent (greater relevant abilities, will power, nerve, fewer moral scruples, and so on). Therefore, those whose murder attempts succeed tend to be more dangerous, on average, than those whose murder attempts fail. Also, given that criminals often commit further crimes, an extra year in jail for a more dangerous criminal better protects the public from repeat

offenses than an extra year in jail for a less dangerous offender. It therefore makes sense to shift jail time from unsuccessful to successful attempters.

But if these are good arguments, should consequentialists advocate that only successful attempts be punished (with 20 years of jail time) and unsuccessful attempts not be punished at all?

‟*In order for something to be a punishment, must there be an ending to it? Hell, many say, is a punishment. But isn't the purpose of punishment to try to make someone realize that what he did was wrong, and to make him a better person? If this is right, then an eternity in hell couldn't be punishment, because those in hell would never get out and be faced with an opportunity to be a better person.*”

Allen Stairs:

A good question! As it turns out, not everyone agrees that the purpose of punishment is to reform people. In fact, some philosophers (Kant is perhaps the foremost) held that the only justification for punishment is that the person deserves it, and if we punish for the sake of making someone better, we fail to show proper respect for that person—we manipulate him for our own ends.

Setting the question of hell aside for the moment, we can see that the argument you raise, if correct, would also count against capital punishment. But whatever one's views on the rightness of capital punishment, the widespread support it has in some places makes clear that many people see punishment as a matter of giving people what they deserve rather than reforming them. This idea, fleshed out and elaborated, is often called the *retributive* theory of punishment, though it's important not to confuse retribution with revenge. Retributive theorists would maintain that the punishment must always be *proportional* to the crime, and so excessive punishment—say, sentencing a petty thief to 20 years in prison—would be wrong. Kant went further. He insisted that even in executing a murderer, we must respect his humanity. "His death ... must be kept free from all maltreatment that would make the humanity suffering in his person loathsome or abominable," Kant wrote. Whether executing someone is consistent with respecting his humanity is open to debate, but Kant insisted that justice demands that the murderer's punishment fit his crime, and hence nothing short of execution will do. Whether we agree or not, what's clear is that the aim of the punishment here is not to make someone a better person, but to serve a particular conception of justice.

But now we can return to your worry about hell, and what we see is that no matter what our view of punishment, it's hard to understand how *anything* a finite human being does could earn him a never-ending stay in hell. In fact, many religious people agree. Not all

believers think that everyone outside of those who confess the proper doctrine are destined for an eternity of
torment. Those who do have a conception of punishment that reformers and retributivists alike are bound
to find puzzling and repugnant.

*"Recently, the Roman Catholic Archdiocese of Los
Angeles was made to pay $660 million to victims of sex
crimes by priests. Since money can't atone for horren-
dous crimes, what's the point of awarding the victims
so much of it? What's the connection between sex abuse
and cash?"*

Thomas Pogge:

I can see three plausible connections.

First, the lives of many of the victims are blighted by
their traumatic experiences. So even if money cannot
undo this damage, it can brighten the lives of the victims. It can do so by enabling them to afford therapy
and counseling, for instance, or simply have a more
worry-free existence in which they don't have to think
twice about a movie ticket or a fancy birthday present
for their children. In such ways, the money makes the
victims' lives less dire than they would otherwise have
been.

Second, there can be great symbolic value in receiving an official acknowledgment and apology. This can be
given without money, to be sure. But if the archdiocese

had been let off with a simple apology, the victims might well have felt that the gravity of the long string of offenses (enabled by decades of official indifference far beyond this archdiocese) had been overlooked. The large sum appropriately symbolizes to the entire country the enormity of the crime—it emphasizes how gravely wrong the church was to allow known pedophiles to feast themselves on children.

Third, the large amount will act as an incentive to greater vigilance. Church officials will do a much better job of self-monitoring if their own privileges and livelihood are on the line. And those who donate money to the church will also be more vigilant because they do not want their money to end up paying for criminal priests' sexual exploits.

"In what sense is being put to death a punishment? How we can talk about things like "suffering" or "loss" if a person is dead?"

Thomas Pogge:

It is true that, once a person has been executed, she is no longer around to suffer the loss of years she might otherwise have lived. But the point of an execution is not to punish the person after she's dead, but before. She is subjected to the experience of living on death row and later to the experience of being killed in the execution chamber; and she must expect all along that many things she cared for are less likely to thrive or to come to fruition.

You might respond that this answer works only for people who know about their impending execution. What about someone who is killed painlessly in her sleep? Could this ever be construed as a punishment? We can give an affirmative answer if we think of punishment in a somewhat extended sense as the setting back of a person's interests. Suppose you have given offense to someone and, in order to punish you, he has been embezzling money from your account. Being an affluent entrepreneur, you never notice the losses (you rather take your business to be less successful than it really is). But, nonetheless, there is a sense in which he really has succeeded in punishing you. Your wealth is something you care a great deal about, and it really has been substantially diminished over time. Similarly, you might be punished by someone who is spreading false rumors about you that damage your reputation among the people who know you, even if no one confronts you with these rumors and you thus remain ignorant of how your reputation has been gravely tarnished.

Once we allow that there can be plausible cases of unexperienced punishments, then it may also be plausible to say that someone is punished after her death by the setting back of interests that were important to her. (After all, if the punishment is not experienced anyway, why should it matter whether the punished person is capable of such an experience at the time of the punishment?) Of course, this is stretching the ordinary notion of punishment a bit, but not, I believe, beyond recognition.

Alexander George:

Most of Thomas' response focuses on your observation that once one is dead one is "not conscious," and he nicely tries to clear a space for the possibility of harm's being done to someone even if that person doesn't feel the harm. But in most of the cases he considers, there is still someone to be the subject of the misfortune: the clueless entrepreneur, for instance, is still around to have his interests set back (even if he's not aware that that is happening).

Death is rather peculiar, however, in that it's a misfortune that eliminates from the world the subject of the misfortune. (Of course, someone's death might be a misfortune for others. But as you note, we put people to death to punish the very people who, if the punishment is carried out, are no longer around.) Once one's dead, not only does one cease to experience things but one ceases to have interests too. That's what makes your question hard. It's really the question the Ancients (and everyone else) argued about: whether someone's death is a misfortune for that person. As one of my students asked when we were discussing this in class, "So murder is a victimless crime?"

Jyl Gentzler:

Of course, murder is not a victimless crime! But how can that be, Prof. George asks, if the victim no longer exists in order to suffer the harm that has been done to him? If you must exist in order to have interests, then how can a dead person's interests suffer as a result of his death?

To see the harm that is suffered by a murder victim, let's think first about what it means to be harmed. If I were to harm Harry, what sort of thing would I have to do him? Intuitively, when I harm Harry, my actions make him worse off than he would have been had I not acted as I did. So when I spread vicious gossip about Harry, I have harmed him because, had I not spread the vicious gossip, his reputation would have been intact, and he would have been well-respected in his community, loved by his family, and able to complete more easily certain projects about which he cares deeply, projects that require the good will and cooperation of others. Because of my vicious gossip, Harry is now a social outcast, unloved and unaided.

So let's try out this definition of harm: *X harms Y if and only if X's action A makes Y worse off than Y would have been had X not performed A.* But now, it seems, we have a problem. If I kill Harry, how can we compare the state that Harry would have been in, had I not killed him, to the state that he's now in, namely, dead? Since he is dead—and we'll suppose for now that if he's dead, he's non-existent—he's in no state at all. How can we compare this "non-state" to his state he would have been in had he been alive?

The answer to this puzzle, I think, is this. If Harry had survived, he would have attained all of the goods that generally come with living: pleasure, deep relationships with others, philosophical knowledge, and so on (complete this list with whatever you count as genuine goods). Of course, had he lived, it's likely that he would have had some hard times, too—some pain, frustration, heart-break, and so forth. But so long as his life would have been worth living, the goods would have outweighed the bads. When I kill Harry, I prevent him from attaining these goods.

When we attempt to figure out the harm that Harry has suffered when I kill him, we should not compare Harry's state after his death to the state that Harry would have been in had I not killed him. For the reasons that I give above, such a comparison is impossible. Instead, when we attempt to figure out the harm that Harry has suffered when I kill him, we should compare the totality of goods that Harry would have had over the entirety of his life, had I not killed him, to the totality of goods that he actually attained in the life that I cut off. If his life would have been worth living, then I did indeed harm Harry when I killed him: I deprived him of all of the goods that he would otherwise have had, had I not killed him.

WAR

"*Is war ever morally permissible?*"

Ernie Alleva:

There surely are intelligent and morally thoughtful individuals who are pacifists, and who believe that going to war is always morally unjustified. However, I think that this view is ultimately unacceptable. I believe that there are circumstances in which going to war would be morally justified—for example, cases of collective self-defense. If one political community is unjustly attacked by another, people can be morally justified in defending themselves against attack by going to war against their attacker. This needn't mean that going to war whenever one is attacked would be morally justified. There may be cases in which the moral costs of self-defense are too high and, thus, would not be justified. But this doesn't count against there being at least some cases in which going to war in self-defense is morally justified.

"*I am in the part-time military, and I may soon be deployed to active service. Can I justify the deaths of any people I am required to kill during operations?*"

Thomas Pogge:

This question cannot be answered in general terms. Some killings that you may be required to perform may be justifiable, others not. Generally, killings in war are thought to be justifiable when two conditions are both fulfilled: Your country must have a just cause for being involved in the war in the first place. And each potentially lethal action within the war must be aimed at a legitimate target while taking great care to spare others who are not a threat. You must reassure yourself on both counts before you start killing people on the orders of others. This can be quite straightforward when you are ordered to defend your country against invading soldiers. But it can be far more difficult, if not impossible, when you are ordered to participate in an attack upon, and occupation of, another country.

" Are military drafts unethical? "

Nicholas D. Smith:

Let me begin by saying that I expect my answer to this one will be controversial, as I think there are deep feelings about this issue, and also a very broad range of considerations. So my own response does not rise above simply stating an opinion for others to consider.

For what it is worth, then: I think that within democracies military drafts should be mandatory. So, I suppose it is obvious that I think they are not unethical in democracies. But within political systems in which the people's consent to government is not given, but rather coerced—the obvious example being dictatorships—military conscription is almost always unethical.

In democracies I think that military drafts should be mandatory and universal, and that exceptions should be made only for medical reasons or extraordinary hardship. The recent situation in which the United States finds itself gives a fairly clear ground for why I say this. It is simply far too easy for a government or regime to become involved in a war when that decision puts at risk only people who have volunteered for the military. If being in the military were instead a matter of civic duty, then the entire citizenry (including especially the families and friends of conscripts!) would be much less eager to have its country go to war. As our fiasco in Iraq shows all too well, we should have been much more reluctant, as a nation, to get into this war. But when it was only volunteers whose lives were going to be lost, well...it was just too easy for the rest of us (many of us with a deep sense of unease notwithstanding) to sit idly by and just allow our government to make this decision for us. Well, the wrong decision was made, and I think such decisions would be much more difficult to make if more people felt what was at stake.

A nation should be prepared to go to war only if and when the case for risking young lives—even those dear to us—is recognized by the majority of the citizens. I think that fewer people would have supported this foolish and reckless war if the stakes included risks to them or to their loved ones, and not just to those who, for whatever reasons, volunteered to risk their lives in the military. (The fact that such reasons are often economic raises very serious questions of equality.)

The USA withdrew from the Vietnam War because that war, another reckless adventure, put too many conscripts' lives at risk, and the American public finally would not put up with having its loved ones killed or maimed without adequate cause. After that war, our politicians' "wisdom" conceived the all-volunteer army precisely because it gave them increased capacity for military engagement without the resistance of the families and loved ones of conscripts. But this resistance is precisely what should be in place to hold in check a too-great readiness to engage in war.

Few thought the draft was immoral during either of the World Wars. That is because there were extremely good reasons to be involved in those wars. But after Vietnam and Iraq, the idea of being conscripted gives us all the creeps. It should give us the creeps! But that same reaction would impede hawkish lawmakers from expensive and deadly wars that do no credit to our country, and waste too many lives (at home and abroad) for poor or selfish reasons.

So it reduces to a simple question: Would we be so willing to vote for a candidate who wished to extend this war "as long as it takes" if it was our own son or daughter who might be the next to die or be terribly injured there? I think not, and if we went back to having the draft, we'd find our current follies ended with alacrity and conviction, and our capacity to make the same mistakes again sharply constrained.

" *Whether one adopts a deontological or consequentialist account of ethics, it is apparent that there exists a moral imperative to prevent genocide. To what extent and to what cost this imperative must motivate our actions is, I suppose, a subject of serious debate. But how can we define genocide? Surely we can all agree that the murder of 10,000,000 people constitutes genocide. But what if we subtract one fatality? Still genocide, of course. Minus one more? The same is still true. But at some point that logic fails; when we get down to the death of one, a few, or no people we certainly no longer have a case of genocide on our hands. If the number of people killed is ultimately arbitrary, how is the concept of genocide meaningful? Surely we can still find moral value in preventing the deaths of millions (or even in the death of an individual), but it seems the label is ultimately kind of subjective and meaningless.* "

Thomas Pogge:

The number of victims is not the only consideration entering into the judgments of whether a genocide is taking place. Other relevant factors are the nature and size of the victim group and the motivations and intentions of the perpetrators. Still, we can hold these other factors fixed and ask your question again, for example: hypothetically lowering the number of people killed, maimed, raped, and otherwise brutalized in the Rwanda genocide, when do we reach the point at which the genocide label would no longer be applicable? Or: At what time, in those horrible months of early 1994, did the daily decision of the world's leading governments not to intervene become a decision to ignore a genocide?

You're right that there is some vagueness here. But this does not render the term meaningless. As Wittgenstein writes, there may be some unclarity about where exactly the boundary lies between two countries—say between China and Russia—but this does not entail that it's unclear on which side Beijing or Moscow falls. Something similar holds true for many terms widely used in the criminal law, terms like "negligent," "reckless," "due diligence," "reasonable person," and so on. Even the word "kill," which you seem to find unobjectionable, is subject to a Sorites problem. Suppose you hurt someone and, as a result, she dies earlier than she would otherwise have done. Have you killed her? Surely yes, if she dies within seconds of your action. Presumably no, if she lives another 80 years rather than 81. So how long exactly must she survive for you to escape the killer label?

We confront and resolve such questions all the time in legislation and jurisprudence, and the borderlines are surely arbitrary to some extent. Here "genocide" is basically in the same boat with lots of other terms and, if we tossed all those terms overboard, we'd have very little language left.

" *Many Americans maintain that, while they oppose the Iraq War, they nonetheless support the troops. But is there really any distinction between support for the war and support for the troops? And what would be the grounds for such a moral distinction? The USA has an entirely volunteer army, so isn't a citizen who joins the military just as guilty of atrocities committed abroad as army and government officials?* "

Oliver Leaman:

No, he isn't just as guilty as the government unless he commits the atrocities or directs that they be committed. When one joins an organization one does not necessarily agree with everything that the organization does. Soldiers should not follow orders that are immoral, and if it is widely believed by them that the enterprise on which they are engaged is immoral or is full of immoral actions, then they should not be a part of it. But in my experience most of the military are not engaged in anything that could be described as immoral or as involving atrocities, and so there is no reason for their non-participation in the war.

Jonathan Westphal:

Is it possible to oppose a war and yet support the troops? If I support the war, that means I believe the ends are justified and good, the means are appropriate, and so on. So I believe in the mission, as you might say. What does it mean to "support the troops"? It might mean that I write comforting letters to people in the services, that I have positive feelings towards the soldiers, that I applaud their representatives on the 4th of July, and so on. These two activities are very clearly different, as the support has two different objects, and so there plainly is a distinction here. The more serious question is whether it is morally *permissible* to engage in the second activity (supporting the troops) without the first (support for the war), especially if we think the war is positively wrong.

Here's an extreme case: Was it morally permissible for good Germans to support the Wehrmacht, the regular army, even if they did not support Hitler and his stated aims? It seems to me that the answer to this question hinges on just how bad the war is thought to be. Supporting the troops if the war is believed to be a great moral evil is itself wrong. But there is nothing wrong with supporting the troops in a war that is believed to be a justified and good one, such as (from the Allied side) the Second World War. So for Americans today the question of whether we should support the troops but not the war depends on just how bad we think the war is. My own view, for what it is worth, is that the war is very bad (even though it appears to be the result of incompetence and lack of intelligence rather than of malice), but not quite bad enough to justify withdrawing our support, if we wish to give it, to people in the services.

"*Is it ethical for the civilized nations of the world to research and stockpile weapons of mass destruction—chemical and biological—for the purposes of warfare? Both Russia and America have stockpiles of smallpox, a deadly virus that could do considerable damage to humanity. Is it ethical to keep said stockpiles as a precaution, as a counter measure to terrorists and warlike nations?*"

Lorraine Besser-Jones:

From an ethical standpoint, the research and development of weapons of mass destruction is justifiable only by appeal to the deterrent effect possession of such weapons has. When a country has weapons of mass destruction, others are deterred from using force against that county. There is a significant catch, though: In order to attain the desired deterrent effect, other countries have to believe that the country who possesses the weapons will, in fact, use them if provoked.

And this is where the logic of deterrence gets sketchy: Ethical considerations of the efficacy of deterrence support the having of weapons, yet in order to serve as deterrents, a country has to be prepared to use them. Those very same ethical considerations, however, may not support the actual use of weapons of mass destruction.

These considerations do not directly respond to one of your central concerns, which is whether or not the use of weapons of mass destruction is justifiable. Yet I do hope to have raised some doubts about inferring the fact that a country is willing to use weapons from the fact that they are researching and developing them. It could be ethical to research and develop them, and yet, at the same time, not be ethical to use them.

THE NATURE OF
MORALITY

MORAL TRUTH

"Does morality truly exist? What if all actions are just self-motivated and "morality" is merely a term we place on these actions to make ourselves feel good, when in fact it doesn't exist?"

Miranda Fricker:

I think one has to ask oneself what it would be for morality to "truly exist." Most ethicists would perhaps agree that morality could not consist of facts or properties that (in J. L. Mackie's phrase—see his *Ethics: Inventing Right and Wrong*) are part of "the fabric of the world." That's to say, few people would argue that morality consists of facts or properties that are out there in the world and detectable by any human being regardless of their sensibility. But maybe there's room for the idea of moral facts and properties on a metaphysically more modest construal. Compare social facts, such as legal facts. Surely the law exists, and it can be a fact that it's illegal to steal, or park your car on the sidewalk, or whatever. These are objective matters about which one can be right or wrong: If one believes that it's lawful to steal, for example, one believes something false. Some such laws may be little more than local conventions; others may be universal, deriving from deep-seated features of human nature (consider laws against murder, or incest). This is just one model of morality that would render it an objective enterprise about which one can make mistakes, but without any suggestion that moral facts are independent of a certain context or point of view.

"Is it possible to have an empirical theory of ethics?"

Peter Lipton:

Moral questions typically have an empirical component. For example, the question whether we have an obligation to paint all the roofs in the world white depends in part on the question whether doing this would reduce global warming, and that is an empirical question. And if Utilitarianism is correct, then you can work out what is right across the board by answering the empirical question of what would generate the most happiness. But the question whether Utilitarianism (or any other ethical theory) is correct does not seem to be an empirical question. What experiment would help? So while *applying* an ethical theory to determine what is right may depend on empirical evidence, whether an ethical theory is correct does not seem to be an empirical matter. The empirical facts only take us so far when it comes to determining what we ought to do.

"Is the statement "it is wrong to torture innocent people for fun" logically necessary in the same sense as "2 + 4 = 6"? Could there, in principle, be a universe that functioned according to completely different moral laws?"

Allen Stairs:

Your question makes most sense on the assumption that there can be objective moral truths; if there can't, then no universe "functions" in accord with any moral laws. So let's assume, at least for the moment, that there are such things as objective moral truths. And now let's make a distinction. Let's agree that as things stand, it's wrong to use Taser guns on babies. Could there be a universe where it was perfectly acceptable to Taser a baby? If we suppose that babies are wired differently in that universe, the answer could well be yes. Perhaps the nervous systems of babies in this distant universe are set up so that applying the Taser provides some sort of painless and beneficial stimulation. And so something that's wrong in our circumstances would be right in that far-off world, but only because some background non-moral facts differ.

Now it may be that background facts about our social arrangements and our ways of understanding our own actions are among the background facts that make a moral difference. A trivial example: In a culture where belching is a way to compliment one's host, it's just fine to belch after a good meal. It's a merely contingent fact that as our society (or mine, in any case) developed, belching at the dinner table would be a way to insult one's host. What we actually happen to care about, value, and abhor is a complicated matter of fact, and on the view I'm interested in, non-moral facts of all sorts can be relevant to right and wrong.

That said, however, could there be two universes that were alike in all these non-moral ways and yet differed on what's right and wrong? Could the moral facts vary independently of all else? I'll confess that I can't see how. And so I'd say: If there are objective moral facts, the most plausible view is that they "supervene" on other sorts of facts. What that means is that there can't be a difference at the level of moral truth without there being a difference in the non-moral facts. Putting it another way, it's plausible that once all the non-moral facts are fixed, all the moral facts are fixed as well.

Of course, if there are no objective moral facts, none of this is so. But then, if there are no objective moral facts, the answer to your question is *no*, because the universe doesn't function according to any moral laws in the first place.

A footnote, however: I'm a little uncomfortable with the phrase "function according to moral laws," because it suggests that moral truths are like physical laws, and that seems to me not to be the right picture. But that's another story, and a long one at that.

"*Many thought experiments in ethics involve truly bizarre scenarios. For instance, the philosopher Frances Kamm talks about putting $500 into a machine that saves children. Do you think that overly contrived examples, too far removed from ordinary experience, lead us in the wrong direction and should not be used? Or should a rigorous philosophy of ethics account for all scenarios, including ones that almost certainly will never occur?*"

Thomas Pogge:
The answer depends on what you take morality— that which moral philosophers are seeking to pin down—to be.

Some philosophers take morality to be a timeless system of norms and values that covers all agents in all possible worlds. Others take morality to be a pragmatic construction that helps human contemporaries to settle their differences peacefully. (These are not the only two options, to be sure, but they are indicative of a spectrum of extant conceptions of morality.)

On the former conception of morality, even the most bizarre imagined intelligent life forms can furnish examples and counter-examples. On the latter conception, even the question what our obligations would be if there were only 5 million human beings living on this planet might be rejected as irrelevant and distracting on the ground that the world is not, and will never again be, so thinly populated. Note that the difference between the two conceptions of morality I have distinguished concerns the larger life world or life context in which actions, decisions, and social institutions are embedded. Thus, the second conception of morality does not easily exclude very unlikely imagined scenarios placed into our familiar life context. The case from Kamm you mention is, I think, of this type. You can imagine child-saver machines to be available in the world as we know it, and by thinking about such a scenario, you can learn something about our obligations to distant children. In particular, Kamm's imaginary scenario helps us think about the obligations that really existing people in affluent countries have toward really existing children in poor countries by separating our doubts about the reliability and effectiveness of available vehicles for aid (such as UNICEF and Oxfam) from our doubts about whether affluent people really have strong obligations of this sort. I am guessing here that Kamm introduces the imaginary machine as a way of focusing on the latter doubts: As a vivid way of asking her readers to assume, for the sake of the argument, that the money we might give would certainly be effective in saving needy children.

Allen Stairs:

While agreeing with everything in Thomas's characteristically clear-headed response, I would add just one note that may bear on your worry. There are philosophers who think that if a thought experiment is too far from our ordinary experience, then our intuitions about what we should say about the case may be unreliable. For example, to take a case from the philosopher Judith Thomson's famous paper on abortion, do we *really* know what our moral views would be if people seeds floated around in the air and could give rise overnight to embryos by lodging in the fabric on your couch? It has also been claimed that some of the more bizarre thought experiments in the personal identity literature suffer from this sort of flaw. We're being asked to decide what would be true if certain very strange circumstances held, when our usual range of experience may not provide us with a thick enough understanding of the relevant "possible worlds" to know what we should say. That said, as Thomas's reply points out, some seemingly bizarre thought experiments are simply meant to help us to ignore irrelevant issues rather than to make sense of worlds well beyond our ken.

“ *Not so many centuries ago, slavery and sexism were morally correct. Now we think they are not correct, and we frown on them severely. Are the changing notions of morality a question to be explored by philosophy, or do they belong to the field of social history?"*

Thomas Pogge:

You need to distinguish between the question of what *is* morally right/wrong and the question of what *is generally taken to be* morally right/wrong at some specific time. Slavery was never morally correct, but at some points in time it was generally taken to be so. (Compare: The earth was never actually the center of the universe, but merely generally taken to be so.)

The first question belongs to philosophy; philosophers try to work out what is morally right/wrong, just/unjust, etc. The second question is addressed by many different disciplines: by social historians, as you say, but also by anthropologists, sociologists, economists, psychologists, brain physiologists, evolutionary biologists, and others as well. Philosophers have addressed it in some of these ways—e.g., Marx within his theory of history and Nietzsche from a psychological perspective in his *Genealogy of Morals*.

"*Since philosophy is a product of Greco-Christian culture, are all its conclusions circumscribed by a tacit limitation ("true only for Westerners"), particularly, perhaps, in the field of ethics?"*

Mitch Green:

Thank you for your question. First of all, it is not true that philosophy is a product of Greco-Christian culture. There are Buddhist, Chinese, and Islamic philosophies (among others) that are not products of Greco-Roman culture. While these philosophies are not as well known in the West as the traditions that trace back to Greek thought, they are complex, innovative, and fascinating traditions in their own right.

But second, and more important, it is hard to see why being a product of a culture would circumscribe a field's conclusions. For instance, it would not be terribly convincing to argue that since Pythagoras was Greek, his Theorem only applies to a certain culture or tradition. Instead, it seems a lot more plausible that his Theorem applies to right triangles no matter which culture you contemplate them from. If this is right, then *just* the fact that a person of a certain culture makes a claim, does not show that his or her claim is only valid within a certain domain. At the very least, more needs to be said to explain why the claim in question only holds within certain limits.

Might the situation be any different for the case of ethics? Insofar as ethics attempts to answer such questions as "What makes right acts right?" and "What sort of character is virtuous?," it attempts to provide answers that transcend any given culture. Ethicists do not in general try to say what it is for a modern urban Westerner to act rightly; rather, they widen the scope of their inquiry to all people no matter the time, location, or cultural milieu. Of course, this makes their inquiry very hard, and it's certainly an occupational hazard of ethics to generalize from one's own parochial conditions to theories of right action across the board. That's an ever-present danger, and many ethical theories have foundered as a result of their author's not having done his or her anthropological homework. This, however, doesn't show that the task is impossible. At most it shows it's very hard to produce sufficiently general ethical theories. My main point, however, is that there seems no reason in principle why an ethical theory *must* be parochial in the way you worry about. If we come across some ethical theories that are, I suspect our conclusion should be: Keep trying!

"*On a TV program tonight, a legal show, the client was a clergyman accused of indecent exposure. He admitted his guilt to the barrister, but said that he was going to plead "not guilty." The barrister replied that under these circumstances he could no longer represent the clergyman. The latter replied "Oh, when did lawyers begin to occupy the high moral ground?" The barrister replied "Probably when the Church first began to confuse morality with ethics." I don't understand what the difference is between morality and ethics. Could the philosopher on duty help with this?*"

Allen Stairs:

Our department was having a meet-and-greet a few months ago. A man came up and said to me in a *you'd better get it right* tone of voice: "What is the difference between morality and ethics?" I told him that in my experience, philosophers don't make a sharp distinction in the way they use those words. I told him that some people seem to use the word "ethics" to talk about what we might call "descriptive morality"—what people happen to think is right or wrong, and reserve the word "morality" for what really *is* right or wrong. But I reiterated that philosophers don't seem too worried about which word we use for what, and many use the words interchangeably.

He told me I was wrong. I behaved myself, and stifled the urge to say "Then why on earth did you ask if you already know the answer?!" But I never did figure out what he meant. My guess about the putdown you describe is that it has to do with a curious association: In certain circles, there's a tendency to think of sex when the word "morality" comes up. Immorality ends up getting reduced to sexual shenanigans of one sort or another. But that's only a guess.

MORAL KNOWLEDGE

"*What reason do we have to believe that our understanding of morality is better now than it was 200 years ago (as opposed to just different)? What is the standard against which moral progress is gauged?*"

Richard Heck:

Here's a simple-minded answer to this question, but that doesn't mean it's not right.

Consider the question whether women should have rights equal to men's. Two centuries ago, this would not widely have been accepted, whereas nowadays it is, at least in Western cultures. So what reason do we have to believe that our understanding of this particular moral question is better than that of our ancestors? That is: What reason do we have to believe that, when we say that women's rights ought to be the same as men's, we are right, and when they said that women's rights ought not to be the same as men's, they were wrong? It seems pretty clear that this is just the question what reason we have to believe that women should have rights equal to men's. I take myself to have *plenty* of reason to believe that.

I think if you asked what reason we have to believe that our understanding of the nature of the physical world is better now than it was 200 years ago, I'd have to give pretty much the same answer.

"*There is increasing evidence that there is an evolved "moral grammar" in human brains. Certain moral beliefs, like the belief that pain is bad and the belief that we should take care of our families, seem to be "hardwired" in us. So while we think that we believe them on some rational basis, we actually believe them because evolution favored those who held them. How is it possible to have a moral system that is rational, when so many of our beliefs are hardwired in this way? These questions leave me in some doubt about the viability of moral philosophy, since all moral theories seem to include premises that I have no reason to accept.*"

Matthew Silverstein:

You pose one of the great challenges confronting philosophical ethics: Explaining the rational basis of morality. If your last claim—that all moral theories include premises you have no reason to accept—is correct, then I don't see how the challenge can be met. A number of philosophers have rejected this claim, however. Kant, for example, suggested that morality is grounded in premises you are rationally bound to accept. According to Kant, simply being a free agent requires you to accept the rational force of certain imperatives, and these imperatives then provide the basis or foundation of your moral obligations.

Note that if Kant is correct, what grounds morality is not any biological fact about the ways in which our brains are hardwired. Rather, it is the metaphysical nature of rational agency that lies at the foundation of ethics. Consequently, *any rational agent*—human or otherwise—will be bound by the same obligations that bind you and me.

Of course, it is not at all clear whether Kant's strategy can succeed, and over the years it has had many critics. Some have objected to Kant's claim that there are imperatives we are rationally bound to accept merely in virtue of being free agents. Others have wondered how we could possibly derive the obligations of morality from foundations that seem so bare and minimal. (And still others have just denied that we're free agents.) Nonetheless, I think that if there is to be any answer to your difficult question, it is going to be found by adopting at least a vaguely Kantian approach.

"*If a person hasn't been taught right from wrong, good from bad, acceptable from unacceptable behavior, how responsible is he for his actions? What about when he realizes his "mistake"?*"

David Brink:

It's a common claim in morality and in the law that one can't be held responsible for wrongdoing unless one was able to know that the conduct in question was wrong and was able to regulate one's actions in accordance with this knowledge. This makes a certain kind of normative competence a condition of responsibility. So the question becomes whether not having been taught right from wrong precludes the requisite kind of normative competence. That depends on both the nature of one's upbringing and the sort of moral knowledge required. I doubt that moral responsibility requires that you be taught explicitly not to violate each and every particular rule. Presumably, one should be able to infer some moral rules (e.g. don't cheat investors) from other ones (e.g. don't cheat). And parents aren't the only source of moral education; friends, teachers, employers, public figures, and the law are also important sources of moral instruction. So the fact that Mom and Dad didn't teach Junior the difference between right and wrong on some particular issue doesn't mean that no one did.

Also, some moral truths are arguably more obvious than others. It's probably easier to see the wrongness of cold-blooded murder than it is to see the wrongness of insider trading. So ignorance of some moral rules might be easier to maintain or harder to overcome than that of others. It's another matter if one's upbringing not only failed to provide certain moral information but actually made it difficult or impossible to absorb certain moral rules. Perhaps certain kinds of parental abuse make it more difficult to be empathetic. Of course, that's a psychological, rather than a philosophical, question. But if it were true, it might mean that people who had been subject to certain kinds of abuse by their parents might lack empathy, which is arguably a capacity that is necessary either to recognize when others are harmed or wronged or to be appropriately moved by this recognition. But then such abuse might tend to compromise normative competence as well.

So it's hard to answer your question in the abstract without more details about the wrongdoing involved and the wrongdoer's upbringing. On the one hand, it's certainly conceivable that one's upbringing could have been so deficient or abusive as to preclude the sort of normative competence required for responsibility. On the other hand, there are many sources of moral education, and many sorts of moral facts are not especially recondite, so that wrongdoers don't automatically get off the hook just because their parents weren't moral exemplars. Moreover, normative competence comes in degrees, with the result that we would probably recognize degrees of responsibility and not always insist that wrongdoers be fully responsible or fully excused. If so, having a weak moral education at home might reduce one's responsibility for some kinds of wrongdoing, even if it did not provide a complete excuse.

"*I thought that modern philosophy tended towards the tentative and the open-ended, with the possibility of error always in sight. Yet some philosophers on this site answer questions, usually on moral issues, with an almost dogmatic certainty worthy of Pope Ratzinger. Why is that?*"

Allen Stairs:

Without discussing specific posts (though I dare say I'm one of the people who fit your bill), it might be something like this: Just as some things are pretty clearly true or false, some things are pretty clearly right or wrong. And if the question posed is "first-level" (one that asks about the rightness or wrongness of some particular act or policy) rather than a difficult question about the foundations or nature of morality, then there's not much point in pretending that something is unclear or up for grabs when it doesn't really seem to be.

Suppose the question was whether it's okay for Robert Mugabe to run Zimbabwe the way he does. I may not know what the best meta-ethical theory is, but if I have any moral knowledge at all, I know that what Mugabe is up to is wrong. So why shilly-shally? Indeed, it's tempting to say that anyone who thinks it is okay for Mugabe to wreck his country and ruin the lives of thousands and thousands of people is a moral incompetent.

Is that dogmatic? Only if it's dogmatic to say firmly what there's no good reason to doubt.

Now of course, there's another conversation we might have: Which things are the ones that there's no good reason to doubt? How does that get settled? It's a perfectly good question, and I don't have a good answer. But it's a different kind of question. Compare: Do we have to be able to provide a theory of knowledge before we can make knowledge claims? If so, we're in big trouble.

In general, philosophers are quite happy to doubt things that other people take for granted, and to take seriously the possibility that their own long-cherished views might be wrong. But what some people describe as our "intuitions" about various matters are an important part of the data that philosophical thinking has to make sense of. Sometimes we end up rejecting some of our intuitions, and sometimes we find ourselves compelled to offer arguments for hanging on to them. But even philosophers have to start thinking somewhere, and if what we're thinking about is right and wrong, some cases seem pretty clear.

MORAL THEORIES

"Socrates said, "It is better to suffer evil than to do it." What does Socrates mean? Can a consequentialist make sense of this claim?"

Jyl Gentzler:

Socrates makes this remark in his dialogue the *Gorgias* in a context in which he's arguing against Polus' conception of the good life—that is, the life that is good for the person who is living it. He is not arguing for the greater importance of moral value over prudential value (or what is sometimes called individual well-being); he is arguing that a person who cares solely about his own individual well-being, as Polus does, should be concerned never to do injustice. This is not because he should worry about getting caught, or about the possibility of someone's taking revenge on his unjust actions, but solely because being an unjust person, in itself, is a bad state to be in. It is bad *for the person who is unjust.* In fact, Socrates believes that being a virtuous person is of overriding prudential value. No other thing comes close to virtue in prudential value, and so, whenever one is faced with the choice between being virtuous and not being virtuous—no matter what benefits might result from one's vicious actions—it is *always* in one's own best interest to choose the virtuous course of action.

You ask what a consequentialist should make of this. I am assuming that by "consequentialist" you mean a person who believes that the *moral* value of an action (or policy, or state of character) is to be assessed solely in terms of its effects on the well-being of people (i.e., on *prudential* value). Consequentialists should pay attention to Socrates' surprising thesis for at least two reasons. (1) Anyone who is concerned with well-being, as consequentialists are, should be concerned about what our well-being consists in. On Socrates' view, our well-being depends largely on our virtue, and so consequentialists who are interested in the implications of their own views should be concerned to determine whether Socrates is right. (2) Ultimately, though, Socrates' position, if correct, is difficult to reconcile with consequentialism. Socrates seems to be saying, contrary to the consequentialist, that the prudential value of an action is to be analyzed in terms of its moral value, not the other way around. I myself don't believe that this is precisely what Socrates is saying because I don't attribute to him a notion of moral value that is distinct from prudential value, and so, I think that it would be difficult for him to make sense of consequentialism (or its negation). On my understanding of Socrates, there is simply one question that is of practical significance for each of us: "What sort of life would be most worth living?" Since I can *directly* control only myself and not the actions of others or the forces of nature and happenstance, this question in fact reduces to the question, "What sort of person should I be?"

"*Many people would say that it's nearly always wrong not to act when someone suffers an unnecessary death that could have easily been prevented. For example, it's wrong to watch a child wander onto a busy road and do nothing to stop her because one doesn't want to lose one's place in line at the post office. It really is difficult to see how this could be morally permissible. But many people would also say that they don't feel any moral obligation to donate their spare money to charity. For example, the money that's required for me to have the internet access I need to ask this question could be used to pay for life saving medication that could spare many children in Africa from a needless, painful death. It seems like on the one hand, we're morally obliged to help when we can, but on the other, it's morally permissible not to help even though we can. Is there any way to make these seemingly conflicting beliefs compatible?*"

Jyl Gentzler:

As you may know, the question that you raise has been raised in very similar terms by Peter Singer in his "Famine, Affluence, and Morality" (*Philosophy and Public Affairs* 1, 1972). Singer presents the moral challenge not merely to Utilitarians like himself, but to all of us, who he believes are deeply committed to the following moral principle: "If one can prevent something very bad from happening (like the death of an innocent child) without any significant sacrifice, then one is morally obligated to do so." Singer himself believes that a much stronger moral principle is true, but he believes that all of us will concede the truth of this principle.

He argues that it is this moral principle that explains our sense that it is not merely a nice thing to save a child from drowning right in front of us, but in fact is a moral obligation, even if it would be a slight inconvenience for us to do so. If true, such a moral principle entails that it would be wrong for us to refrain from giving away money that we have good reason to believe could be used to prevent horrible suffering and avoidable early death, when to do so would entail little inconvenience or sacrifice. While distance might make a psychological difference, and so could be appealed to in order to *explain* the difference in our propensity to respond to local drowning children and not to foreign starving children, Singer argues that distance from ourselves makes no more moral difference than skin color. People who are close in space to us are no more deserving of our moral concern than are those who live farther from us. The philosopher Peter Unger argues for a similar position in his book, *Living High and Letting Die.*

Morality is demanding, both of them would insist, and they would reject the suggestion that it is the job of philosophical ethics to avoid a morality that implies perpetual guilt. To the contrary, they maintain that we should all feel a much greater sense of guilt than we do, because we are all guilty of failing to meet our most basic moral obligations.

That said, some Utilitarians have argued, to my mind convincingly, that the best versions of Utilitarianism do not require that we become alienated from the sorts of personal projects and attachments that make it possible for us to live good and meaningful lives. I would recommend the philosopher Peter Railton's "Alienation, Consequentialism, and the Demands of Morality" and "How Thinking about Character and Utilitarianism Might Lead to Rethinking the Character of Utilitarianism," both reprinted in his book, *Facts and Values*.

" *What implications does chaos theory have for consequentialism? It seems that through chaos theory and the "butterfly effect," it is impossible for anyone to know which action is the one that will create the most happiness in the world. There are extreme cases, of course: when you're trying to decide whether to save a child from drowning, you can't possibly know whether the child will grow up to be a good person or a murderer. But even in regular every day cases, each course of action that we contemplate taking has literally billions of results that are impossible to know about. So it seems impossible to know which action is the morally right one. How would consequentialists, such as John Stuart Mill, respond to this worry?"*

David Brink:

Insofar as a system is chaotic, it is impossible to predict all the consequences of some event. Many systems, while not literally chaotic, are still complex, with the result that predictions about the total consequences of one's actions are difficult and not fully reliable. But it's not clear that these facts about complexity and chaos compromise the claims of classical Utilitarians, such as Mill. The classical Utilitarians (e.g., Jeremy Bentham, John Stuart Mill, and Henry Sidgwick) all insisted that Utilitarianism—the demand that we act so as to maximize human happiness—be understood as a *standard* of duty or right action, rather than as a *decision procedure*. That is, what determines the moral assessment of one action in relation to others is the comparative value of its actual consequences, not the comparative value of its expected consequences.

Whether we should try to apply the Utilitarian principle in various contexts is itself a practical question, the answer to which depends upon the comparative consequences of doing so. Calculating utility is time consuming (and so has opportunity costs) and is often subject to ignorance (as in complex or chaotic systems) or bias and distortion (due, for example, to self-interest). For these reasons, we may often do a better job of promoting utility, not by trying to, but rather by adhering to various discrete moral rules that make no direct reference to utility, such as familiar rules about non-aggression, honesty, fidelity, and fairness. Mill called these rules *secondary principles* and insisted that the Utilitarian first principle, which supplied the standard of right conduct, be supplemented by various secondary principles. He thought we should review the value of our secondary principles from time to time, and that we should resolve conflicts among secondary principles by direct appeal to the principle of utility. But otherwise our conduct should be more or less strictly regulated by such secondary principles. Of course, in cases of conflict among the secondary principles, direct appeal to Utilitarian calculation may prove unreliable, due to complexity or chaos. All we can do, it seems, is do our best. This won't determine what is best to do—that's a matter of what *in fact* maximizes utility—but it may mean that what we do is blameless, even if it results in action that is strictly speaking wrong.

"*Although I have read many responses here that demonstrate wisdom, I doubt that the kinds of moral theories often mentioned here—for example, utilitarianism and deontological ethics—have much to do with this wisdom. The theories almost caricature the serious, worried thinking that I have to do about whether, say, I must send my daughter to live with her grandparents in a different country. Not that these theories have got it all wrong. But they make an academic exercise out of a real moral problem, changing it in ways I don't understand but still feel are there. What is the value of moral theories? And what is the point of moral philosophy departments?"*

Lisa Cassidy:

I feel your pain. You like philosophy and want it to be relevant, but when confronted by real-life problems the theories always seem to fall flat.

As you observe, most ethical writing tends to be abstract, removed from actual cases, and too densely packed with fancy terms to be of use. There are major exceptions to that generalization; much of applied ethics or feminist ethics might meet your demands for less speculative and more concrete writing. I recommend both approaches absolutely!

However, I would like to try sticking up for the good old boys (Mill, for example). Even if reading about the "decided preference criterion" might not tell you how to raise your child, Mill might arm you with a helpful set of principles that seem appropriate, or even wise. (Example: if sending my daughter to her grandparents will likely cause more overall good than ill, I ought to do it, even if I personally regret seeing her go.) So I think there is good stuff in ethical theory, stuff worth unearthing, even if the philosophers make you work for it.

As for the institutional trappings of philosophy, it is regretful that philosophy is just another commodity in the academic marketplace—a lowly commodity at that. But philosophers ought to make themselves relevant by showing students, professionals, and lay people that philosophy (if it is done right) can be nothing less than transformative.

PUTTING MORALITY INTO PRACTICE

"In ethics, philosophers spend a lot of time trying to figure out what is moral and immoral. But why should we be moral? Where does this obligation to be moral come from?"

Douglas Burnham:

The answer (which you won't like at all) is this: Morality can be defined roughly as "what I should do." So, asking the question "Why should I be moral?' is equivalent to asking "Why should I do what I should do?" It answers itself, in much the same way as "What colour is that red thing?" answers itself. Well, that's not very interesting.

Much more interesting is the second version of your question: Why is there moral obligation at all? That is the question which, in a hundred variations, has been worrying philosophers for thousands of years. Surprisingly, perhaps, very few philosophers have concluded by saying that there are no moral obligations whatsoever, nor any obligations remotely akin to them. (Even Nietzsche, who is often misunderstood on this point, speaks about virtues and duties as well as concepts like gift-giving and friendship.)

Jyl Gentzler:

I agree that on one understanding of the question "Why should I be moral?," the question is unintelligible. But I think that when most people ask that question, they are asking a question that is short-hand for more substantive questions, like "Why should I tell the truth?," "Why shouldn't I cheat on this exam?," "Why should I refrain from stealing if I can get away with it?," and "Why should I care about anyone other than myself?" Morality, it seems, requires me to restrain my pursuit of my own self-interest for the sake of the interests of others, and I think that it is completely reasonable to ask why I should do that. (It's interesting, I think, that few people feel compelled to answer the question, "Why should I care about myself?")

Different answers have been offered to the question "Why be moral?" Most common (and least plausible, to my mind) is the answer: "Because the Gods want you to." Least common (but most plausible, to my mind) is the answer: "Because by taking seriously the interests of other people you will live the best sort of life that you could possibly live."

"*Could you explain the relationship between intellect and morality? From the questions I read on this site, it seems that many people expect philosophers—obviously smart people—to live morally better-than-average lives. But is there any correlation between being intelligent and acting morally?*"

Louise Antony:

I don't know if there is any general presumption that intelligence and morality go together. And it's up for grabs, I think, whether there is any general faculty of "intelligence," equally applicable to, and equally present in all domains. But suppose we're talking about "school intelligence," the kind of ability that's tested on IQ tests. In that case, I think the following can be said.

If one is basically a good person, or tries sincerely to be, then intelligence can be an aid in acting morally, and in understanding what morality is. It can help you develop a comprehensive and consistent system of moral principles, help you render your judgments

194

consistent, help you think of new cases to test out your principles, and help you keep your thinking straight when matters get complicated. But if you are dishonest, insensitive, selfish, cruel, or negligent, intelligence can be a hindrance to your moral development insofar as it facilitates your constructing clever but bogus rationalizations for your immoral behavior.

Douglas Burnham:

Let us distinguish between knowing why, knowing that, and character. The person who "knows why" is the moral theorist: He or she understands the relationship among principles, the various avenues of justification, the standard arguments and objections, and so forth. Someone who "knows that" has an accurate grasp of what is good, although he or she might not be able to explain why, or even recognize the need to do so. (I won't dwell on what "accurate" might mean here, for the same reason, presumably, as you put "better" into scare-quotes!) "Character" is the capacity (the will, the strength, whatever) to turn moral knowledge into action. Clearly, neither of the first two is any good without the last. Moreover, I see no good reason why the person who "knows why" is any more likely to have a virtuous character than the person who "knows that"—indeed, it might be the reverse.

However, all is not lost. First of all, there may be certain types of moral training that do connect "knowing why" with character. In such a case, moral theory is not a disinterested academic activity, but a way of living. For an obvious historical example, see the last major division of Kant's *Critique of Practical Reason*, entitled "The Methodology of Pure Practical Reason."

Second, people who "know why" may be more likely than those who just "know that" to influence others, and change wider public attitudes.

Third, precisely because moral theory insists on justification, those who "know why" may be less susceptible to the common sense of their era than those who merely "know that."

"*I have a few friends, professional philosophers, who recognize the strength of arguments for vegetarianism, admit that they don't have any good counter-arguments, but still don't turn vegetarian. Is rational argument really persuasive? What is the authority of moral reasoning? Is there something one can do through reason to persuade the sensible knave?*"

Oliver Leaman:

I have friends who are convinced that one should always tell the truth and yet do not do so, and librarians are familiar with the phenomenon that books on ethics seem to disappear with greater frequency than on many other topics. It is one thing to be convinced by an argument, and quite another to make that fact of personal relevance to your life.

This is not just a feature of morality. It occurs also in areas like sports, where we often know what we ought to do to score when taking a penalty kick, for instance, but don't, for one reason or another. And that is the essence of the issue: Other things intervene, such as our habits, who we are with, what image of ourselves we wish to project, and so forth, and they overcome our reasoning on occasion. The world would be much more boring were this not to be the case, of course, since it is in the contrast here between what we want to do and what we know we ought to do that so much of the pleasure of being alive rests.

" To what extent do philosophers, or people who think deeply about an issue, have a responsibility to some kind of direct action, especially in cases like climate change where they perceive a significant threat to the future of humanity?"

Thomas Pogge:

I don't think this responsibility is confined to those who have thought deeply about an issue. If climate change is a menace to the poor today and to future generations, and if we are much involved in fuelling this menace, then we all have a responsibility to act to slow down and stop this phenomenon. If the responsibility were confined to those who have thought deeply about this, the others could easily get off the hook simply by avoiding deep thought.

Still, I agree that those who understand the problem better than most have a special role to play, namely the role of alerting others to their responsibilities. This is something philosophers can do and should do much more of: Help citizens think clearly and critically about their responsibilities as citizens of their state and of the world. In most cases, this indirect way of doing something about the problem is likely to be more effective than direct action. And it has the additional advantage of helping one's fellow citizens avoid being involved in grave wrongs.

BIOGRAPHICAL INFORMATION

Ernie Alleva is Lecturer and Research Associate at Smith College. His main research interests are in moral and political philosophy, including philosophical issues regarding work, contemporary controversies about freedom of speech and expression, and recent work in political theory regarding Rawls' conception of political liberalism.

Louise Antony is Professor of Philosophy at the University of Massachusetts, Amherst. Her current research focuses on perception and intentionality, autonomy of psychology, issues in feminist epistemology, and human nature.

Lorraine Besser-Jones teaches philosophy at Middlebury College. She received her Ph.D. from the University of North Carolina at Chapel Hill, and held positions at Stanford University and the University of Waterloo before moving to Middlebury. She has published articles in moral psychology, Hume's moral philosophy, and just war theory. She is particularly interested in the nature of moral motivation considered from both historical and contemporary perspectives.

David O. Brink is Professor of Philosophy at the University of California, San Diego, Co-Director of the Institute for Law and Philosophy at the University of San Diego School of Law, and editor of the journal *Legal Theory*. His research interests are in ethical theory, history of ethics, and jurisprudence.

Douglas Burnham is Professor of Philosophy at Staffordshire University. His research is centered on Kant, Nietzsche, recent European philosophy, and the relation of philosophy and the arts.

Andrew N. Carpenter is Professor of Philosophy at Ellis University. His specialty is the history of early modern philosophy, especially Immanuel Kant's theoretical philosophy, and he is particularly interested in the practical applications of philosophical ideas and methodologies to individuals' personal and professional lives.

Lisa Cassidy is Associate Professor of Philosophy at Ramapo College of New Jersey. Her research often focuses on the family, personal responsibility, and embodiment, but includes writing on pedagogy and "popular" philosophy as well. She has published articles on who should have children, what charitable obligations exist between strangers, why undergraduates learn philosophy from stick figure drawings, and how the television character Carmela Soprano uses care ethics.

Mark Crimmins is Associate Professor of Philosophy at Stanford University. He is interested in language, mind, and reality.

Roger Crisp is Uehiro Fellow and Tutor in Philosophy at St Anne's College, Oxford, and Professor of Moral Philosophy at the University of Oxford. He is the author of *Mill on Utilitarianism* (Routledge, 1997) and *Reasons and the Good* (Clarendon Press, 2006).

Peter S. Fosl is Professor of Philosophy at Transylvania University in Lexington, Kentucky. Co-author with Julian

Baggini of *The Philosopher's Toolkit* (Blackwell Publishing, 2003) and *Ethics Toolkit* (Blackwell Publishing, 2007), Fosl has published numerous academic works on skepticism, David Hume, and the philosophy of religion. Fosl has also written for non-academics as a contributing editor to *The Philosophers' Magazine* and books such as *Lost and Philosophy* (Blackwell Publishing, 2008) and *Metallica and Philosophy* (Blackwell Publishing, 2007). Fosl earned his Ph.D. from Emory University and was also educated at Bucknell University and the University of Edinburgh. In 2006, he was named the University of Kentucky's Acorn Professor of the Year.

Miranda Fricker is Reader in Philosophy at Birkbeck, University of London. She is the author of *Epistemic Injustice: Power and the Ethics of Knowing* (Oxford University Press, 2007); co-author of *Reading Ethics: Selected Texts with Interactive Commentary*, written with Sam Guttenplan (Wiley-Blackwell, 2009); and co-editor of *The Cambridge Companion to Feminism in Philosophy* with Jennifer Hornsby (Cambridge University Press, 2000). Her main areas of interest are ethics, social epistemology, virtue epistemology, and those areas of feminist philosophy that focus on issues of power, social identity, and epistemic authority.

Jay L. Garfield is Doris Silbert Professor in the Humanities and Professor of Philosophy at Smith College. He is also Professor in the Graduate Faculty of Philosophy at the University of Massachusetts, Professor of Philosophy at Melbourne University (Australia), and Adjunct Professor of Philosophy at the Central Institute of Higher Tibetan Studies (India). He teaches and pursues research in the philosophy of mind, foundations of cognitive science, logic, philosophy of language, Buddhist philosophy, cross-cultural hermeneutics, theoretical and applied ethics, and epistemology.

Jyl Gentzler is William R. Kenan, Jr. Professor of Philosophy at Amherst College. She has published several articles on the Socratic method in Plato's dialogue as well as on Plato's conception of the good.

Alexander George is Professor of Philosophy at Amherst College.

Mitch Green teaches at the University of Virginia. His research concerns the philosophy of language, aesthetics, and the philosophy of mind. He also heads the Hi-Phi Project, which explores ways of strengthening philosophical education in high schools.

Sally Haslanger is Professor of Philosophy and Director of the Women's and Gender Studies Program at the Massachusetts Institute of Technology. Her interests are broad, and include analytic metaphysics and epistemology, ancient philosophy (especially Aristotle), social and political philosophy, and feminist theory.

Richard Heck is Professor of Philosophy at Brown University. His interests lie primarily in the areas of philosophy of language, logic, and mathematics.

Amy Kind is Associate Professor of Philosophy at Claremont McKenna College. Her research interests lie primarily in the philosophy of mind, and she has published work on topics such as consciousness, introspection, and the imagination. Her articles have appeared in journals such as *Philosophy and Phenomenological Research, Philosophical Studies*, and *The Philosophical Quarterly*. For fun, she has also recently gotten in touch with her inner science fiction geek by publishing work that addresses the philosophical implications of shows such as *Battlestar Galactica* and *Star Trek*.

Marc Lange is the Bowman and Gordon Gray Distinguished Professor of Philosophy at the University of North Carolina at Chapel Hill. His most recent book is *Laws and Lawmakers: Science, Metaphysics, and the Laws of Nature* (Oxford University Press, 2009).

Oliver Leaman is Professor of Philosophy and Zantker Professor of Judaic Studies at the University of Kentucky. He writes mainly in the areas of Islamic and Jewish philosophy, and his most recent publications are *Islamic Aesthetics: An Introduction* (Edinburgh University Press, 2004), *Islam: The Key Concepts*, co-written with Kecia Ali (Routledge, 2007), and *Jewish Thought: An Introduction* (Routledge, 2006). He is currently working on a book to be entitled *Judaism: An Introduction*, which will be published by I. B. Tauris. Right now he is particularly interested in the links between art and religion.

Peter Lipton (1954–2007) was born in New York City and died in Cambridge, England. He was educated at the Ethical Culture Schools in New York, majored in Physics and Philosophy at Wesleyan University, earned his D.Phil. at Oxford University, and taught at Clark University and Williams College before joining the Department of History and Philosophy of Science at Cambridge University in 1991. He had been Head of Department for seven years when he died after a game of squash, a game he loved. Peter also loved teaching, and would happily engage pedagogically with anyone who wanted to engage with him (and many people did), from members of the Royal Society and the Nuffield Foundation to Cambridge University students, pupils at local high schools, and five-year-olds in synagogue children's services. AskPhilosophers was a great source of pleasure to Peter, and he was full of admiration for the project. Colleagues read out some of his contributions to the website at his memorial service.

Thomas Pogge received his Ph.D. in philosophy from Harvard, and has published widely on Kant and in moral and political philosophy. He is Leitner Professor of Philosophy and International Affairs at Yale University, Professorial Fellow at the Australian National University Centre for Applied Philosophy and Public Ethics, and Research Director at the Oslo University Centre for the Study of Mind in Nature. His recent publications include *Politics as Usual* (Polity Press, 2010); *Hacer justicia a la humanidad* (Fondo de Cultura Económica, 2009); *World Poverty and Human Rights*, 2nd edition (Polity Press, 2008); and *The Health Impact Fund: Making New Medicines Accessible for All*, co-authored with Aidan Hollis (Incentives for Global Health, 2008). Pogge is editor for social and political philosophy for the on-line Stanford Encyclopedia of Philosophy and a member of the Norwegian Academy of Science. His current work is focused on a team effort toward developing a complement to the pharmaceutical patent regime that would improve access to advanced medicines for the poor worldwide (for more information, see www.healthimpactfund.org).

Kalynne Hackney Pudner received her Ph.D. in Philosophy from the University of Virginia, with a specialization in ethical theory. She lives with her husband and nine children in Alabama, where she teaches ethics and philosophy of law at Auburn University. Her primary research interests are family and interpersonal ethics, and the philosophical implications of electronic interaction.

Jasper Reid is Lecturer at King's College London, University of London. He works primarily on early modern philosophy.

Gabriel Segal is Professor of Philosophy at King's College London, University of London. His main interests are in the philosophies of psychology and linguistics.

Matthew Silverstein is Assistant Professor of Philosophy, NYU Abu Dhabi. His is interested primarily in ethics and the philosophy of action.

Nicholas D. Smith is James F. Miller Professor of Humanities and Director of the Classical Studies Program at Lewis and Clark College. His philosophical interests include ancient Greek philosophy (especially Socrates), the philosophy of religion, virtue theory, and epistemology.

Peter Smith is a member of the Philosophy Faculty at the University of Cambridge. He has written books on the philosophy of mind and chaos theory, as well as two logic texts. He edited the journal *Analysis* for twelve years.

Miriam Solomon is Professor of Philosophy at Temple University. Her research interests are in philosophy of science, philosophy of medicine, history of science, epistemology, gender and science, and biomedical ethics.

Allen Stairs is Associate Professor of Philosophy at the University of Maryland. His work has focused on the foundations of quantum mechanics, but he is also interested in the philosophy of religion, the problem of free will, and the pedagogical issues that arise when conveying philosophical ideas to a non-academic audience.

Saul Traiger is Professor of Philosophy at Occidental College. His research includes work on the historical and conceptual foundations of cognitive science, the philosophy of mind, epistemology, and the philosophy of David Hume.

Jonathan Westphal has worked primarily on questions at the intersection of philosophy of mind and metaphysics, especially the philosophy of color. He is also interested in the philosophy of time, human freedom, Leibniz, and poetry. He has been an Alexander Humboldt Fellow at the Institut für Statistik und Wissenschaftstheorie in the University of Munich, and Professor of Philosophy at Idaho State University. His publications include *Colour: A Philosophical Introduction* (Oxford, 1991) and *Philosophical Propositions* (Routledge, 1998).

BIBLIOGRAPHY

SUGGESTED READINGS IN ETHICS

Contemporary Overviews

Marcia Baron, Philip Pettit, Michael Slote. *Three Methods of Ethics: A Debate*. Blackwell Publishers Ltd., 1997.

Simon Blackburn. *Being Good*. Oxford University Press, 2001.

Will Kymlicka. *Contemporary Political Philosophy: An Introduction*. Oxford University Press, 2001.

Michael Sandel. *Justice: What's the Right Thing to Do?* Farrar, Straus and Giroux, 2009.

Russ Shafer-Landau. *The Fundamentals of Ethics*. Oxford University Press, 2009.

Adam Swift. *Political Philosophy: A Beginners' Guide for Students and Politicians*. Polity Press, 2006.

Bernard Williams. *Morality: An Introduction to Ethics*. Cambridge University Press, 1972.

Foundational Texts

Aristotle. *Nicomachean Ethics*. Cambridge University Press, 2000.

Immanuel Kant. *Groundwork of the Metaphysics of Morals*. Cambridge University Press, 1998.

John Stuart Mill. *Utilitarianism*. Oxford University Press, 1998.

John Stuart Mill. *"On Liberty" and Other Writings*. Cambridge University Press, 1989.

Collections of Classical and Modern Readings

Hugh LaFollette, ed. *Ethics in Practice: An Anthology*. Blackwell Publishing, 2002.

Mark Timmons. *Conduct and Character: Readings in Moral Theory*, 5th edition. Wadsworth Publishing, 2005.

SUGGESTED INTRODUCTIONS TO PHILOSOPHY

Kwame Anthony Appiah. *Thinking It Through: An Introduction to Contemporary Philosophy.* Oxford University Press, 2003.

Simon Blackburn. *Think: A Compelling Introduction to Philosophy.* Oxford University Press, 1999.

Thomas Nagel. *What Does It All Mean?: A Very Short Introduction to Philosophy.* Oxford University Press, 1987.

INDEX